TRADITIONAL TATTOO COLORING BOOK FOR KIDS

VOL 1

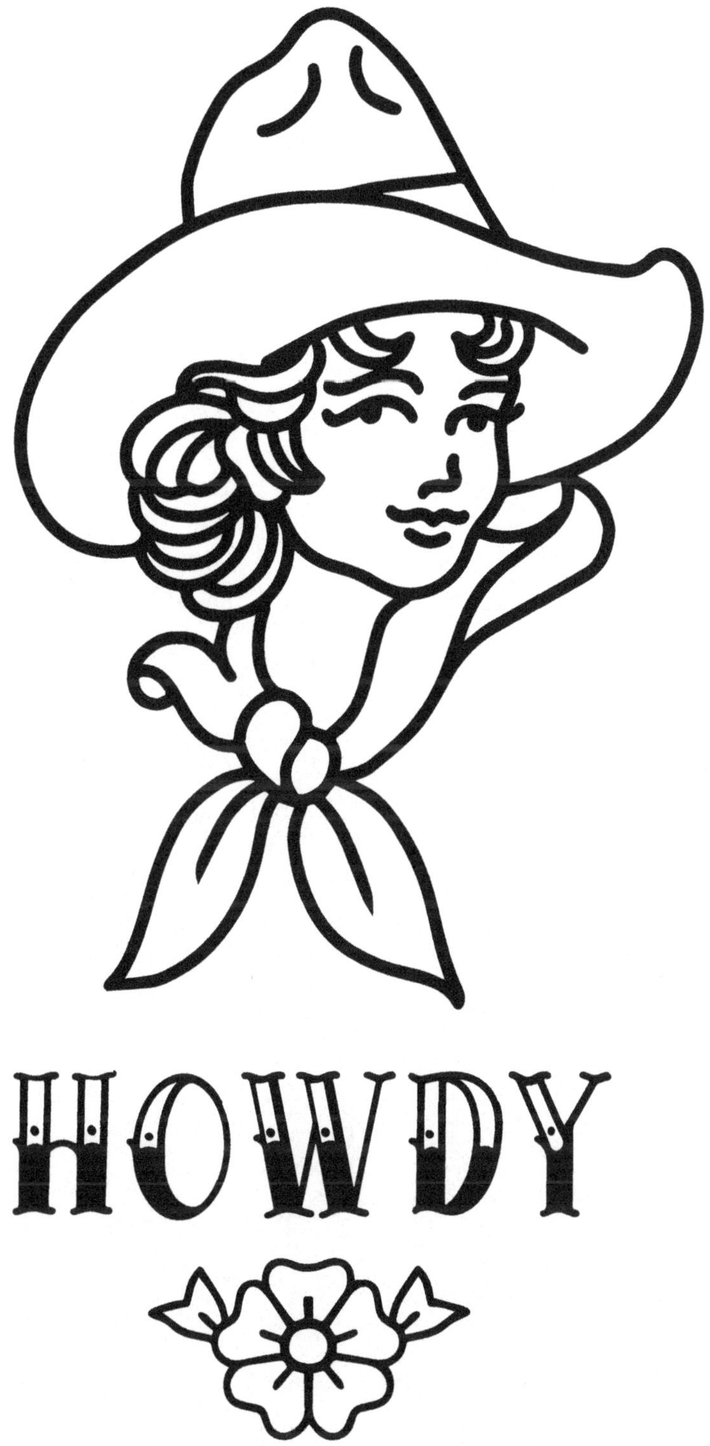
HOWDY

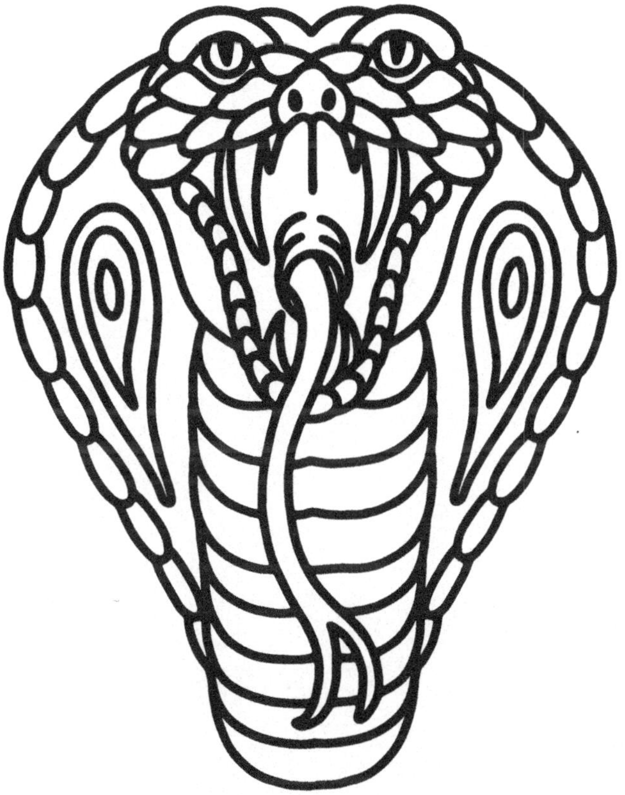

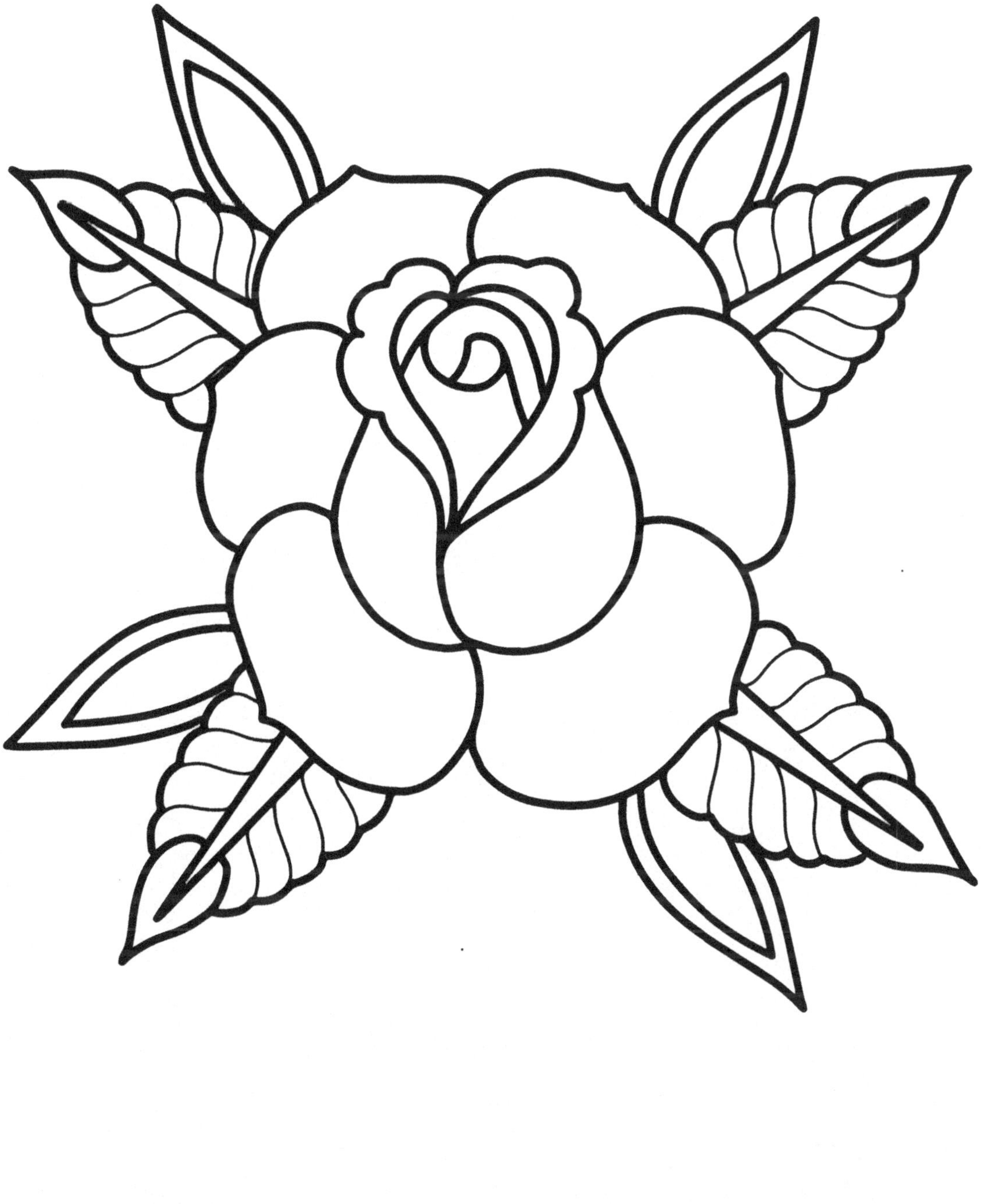

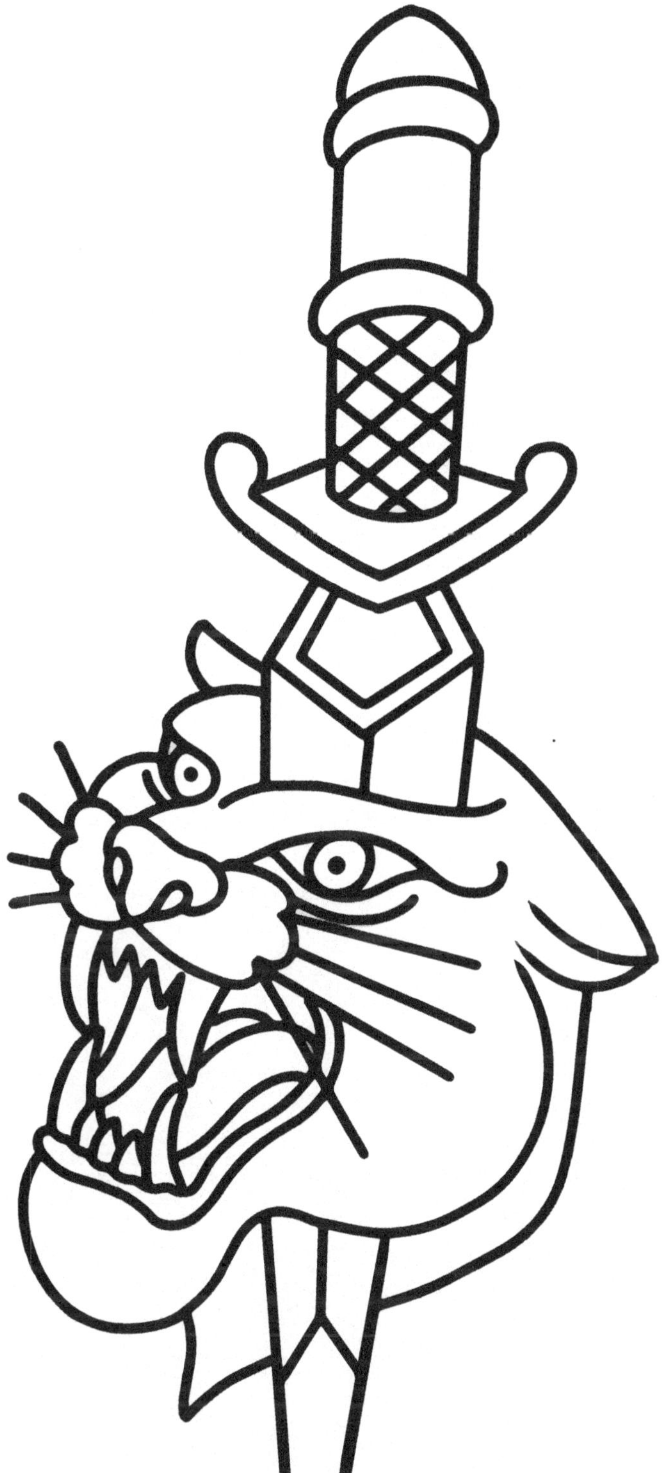

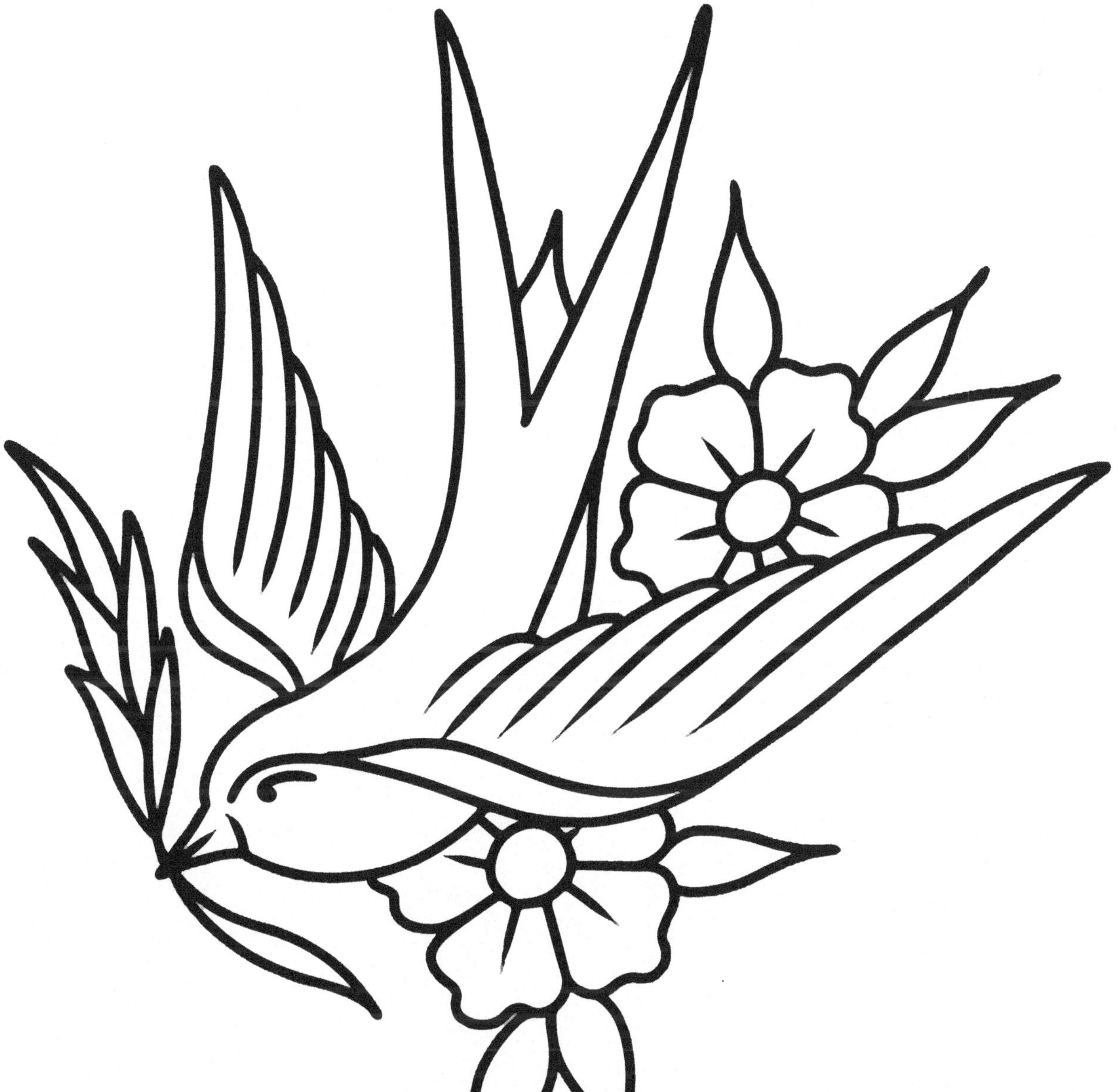

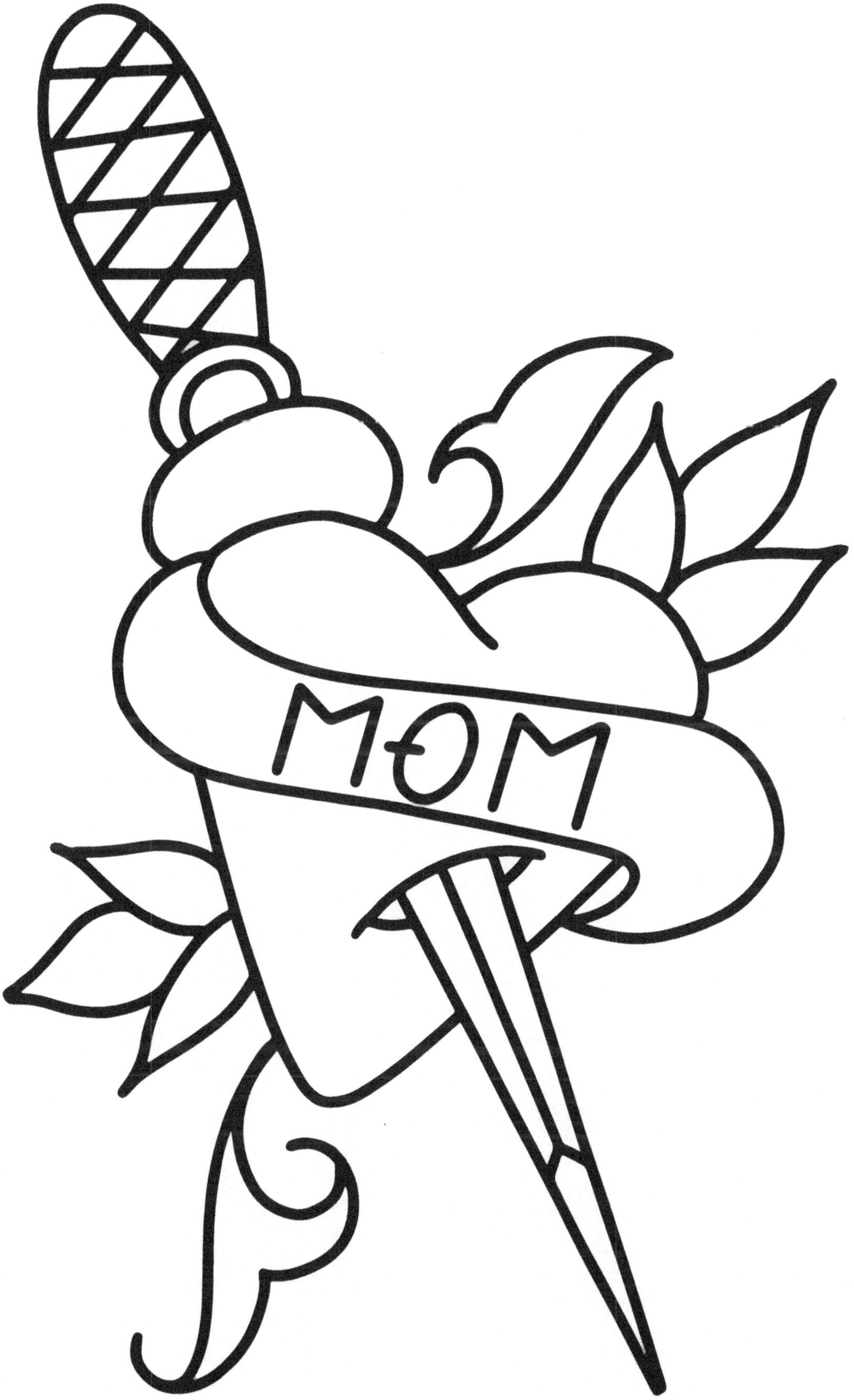
MOM

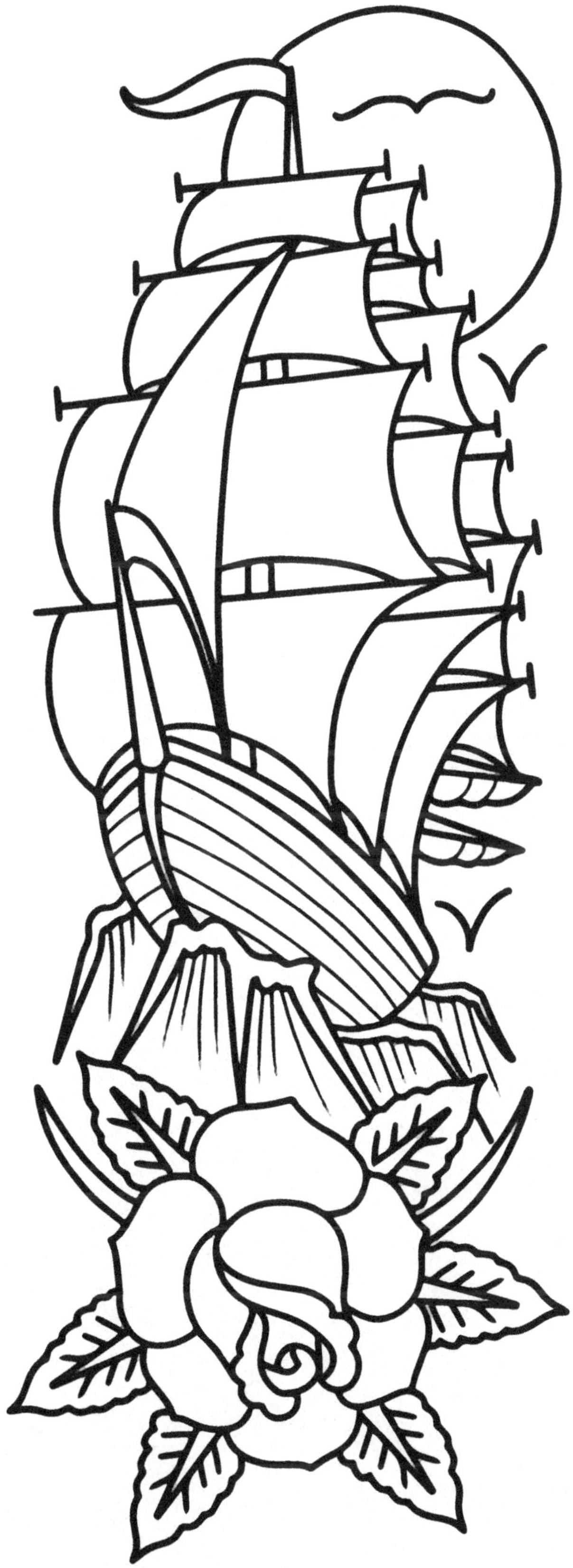

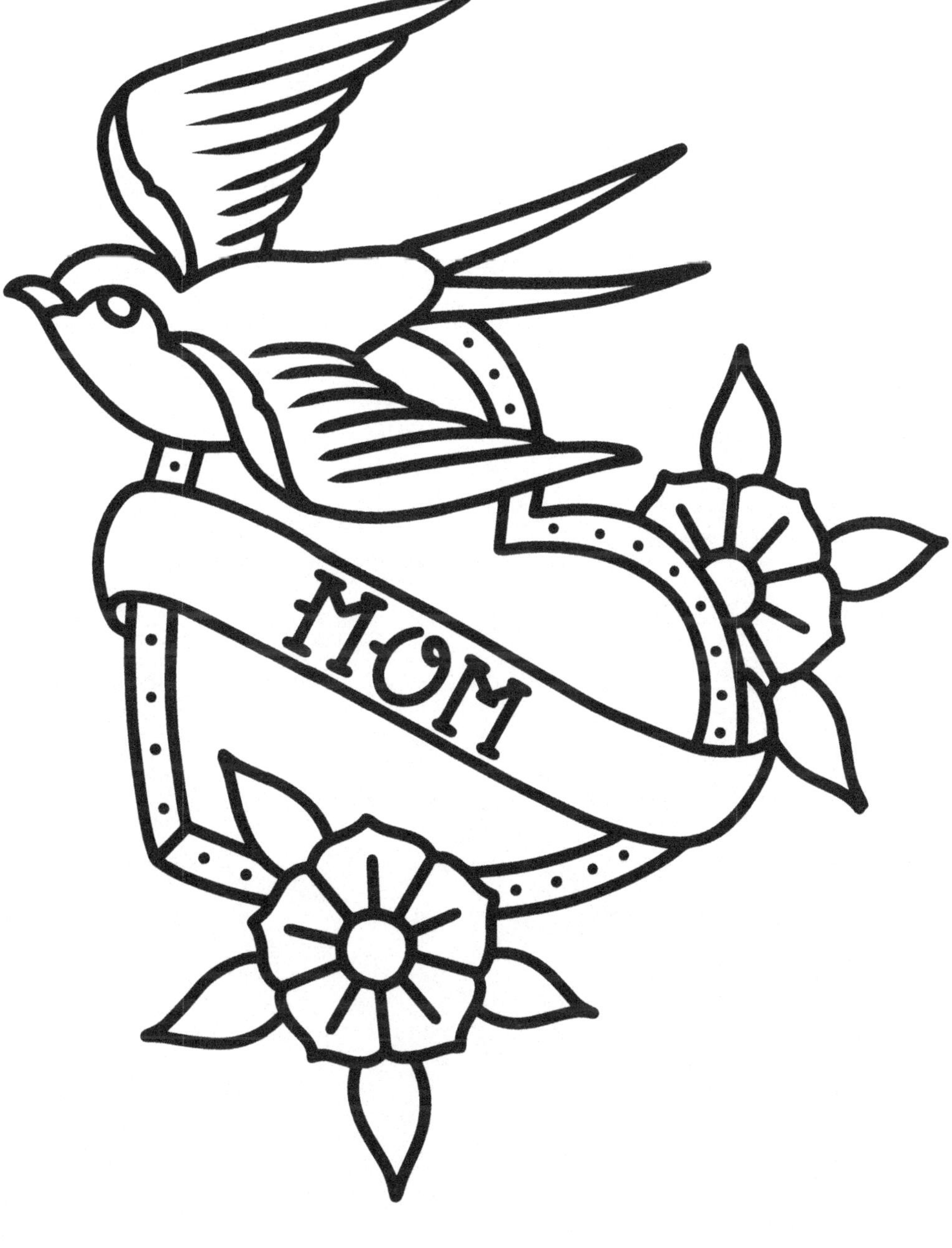
MOM

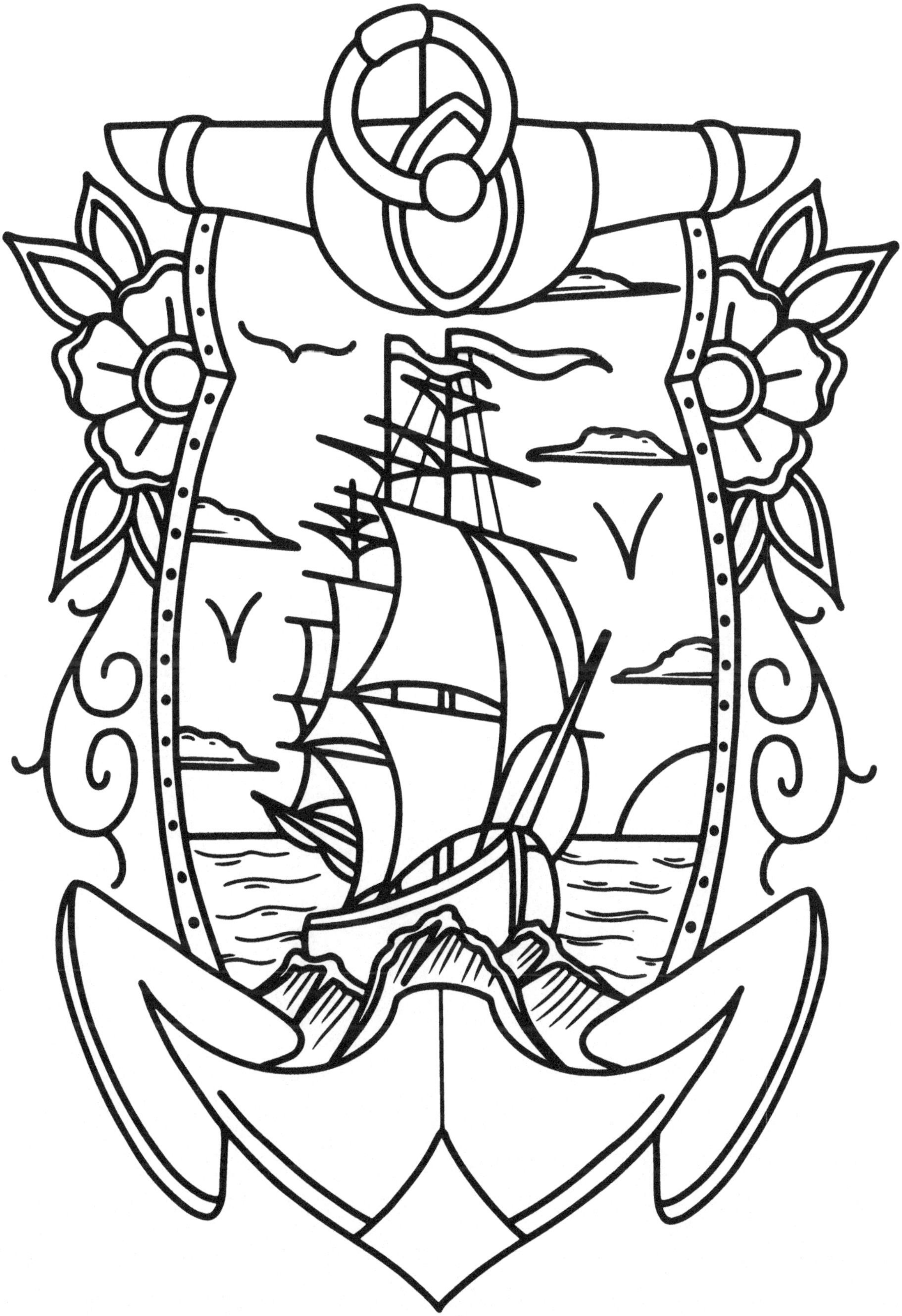

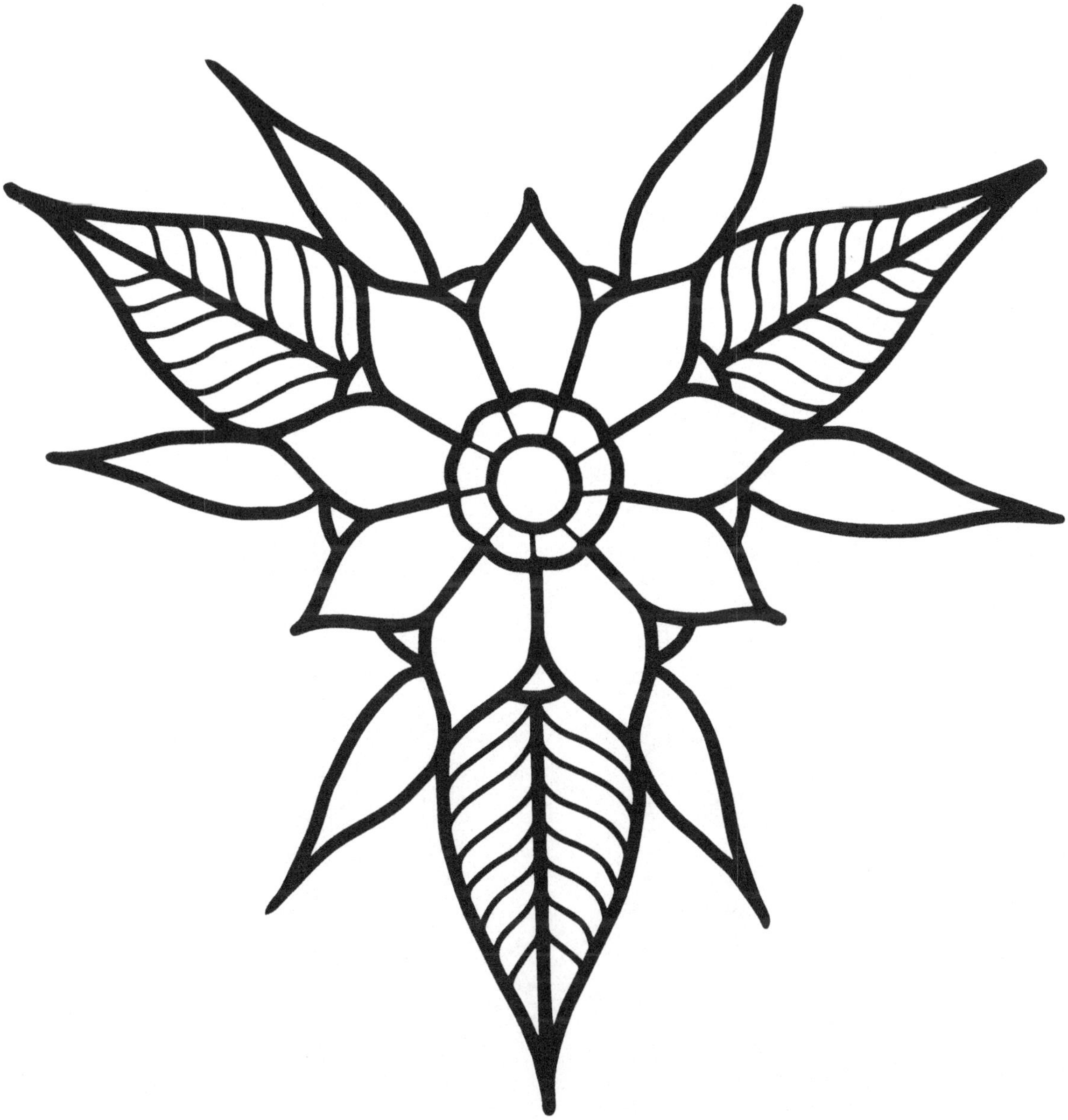

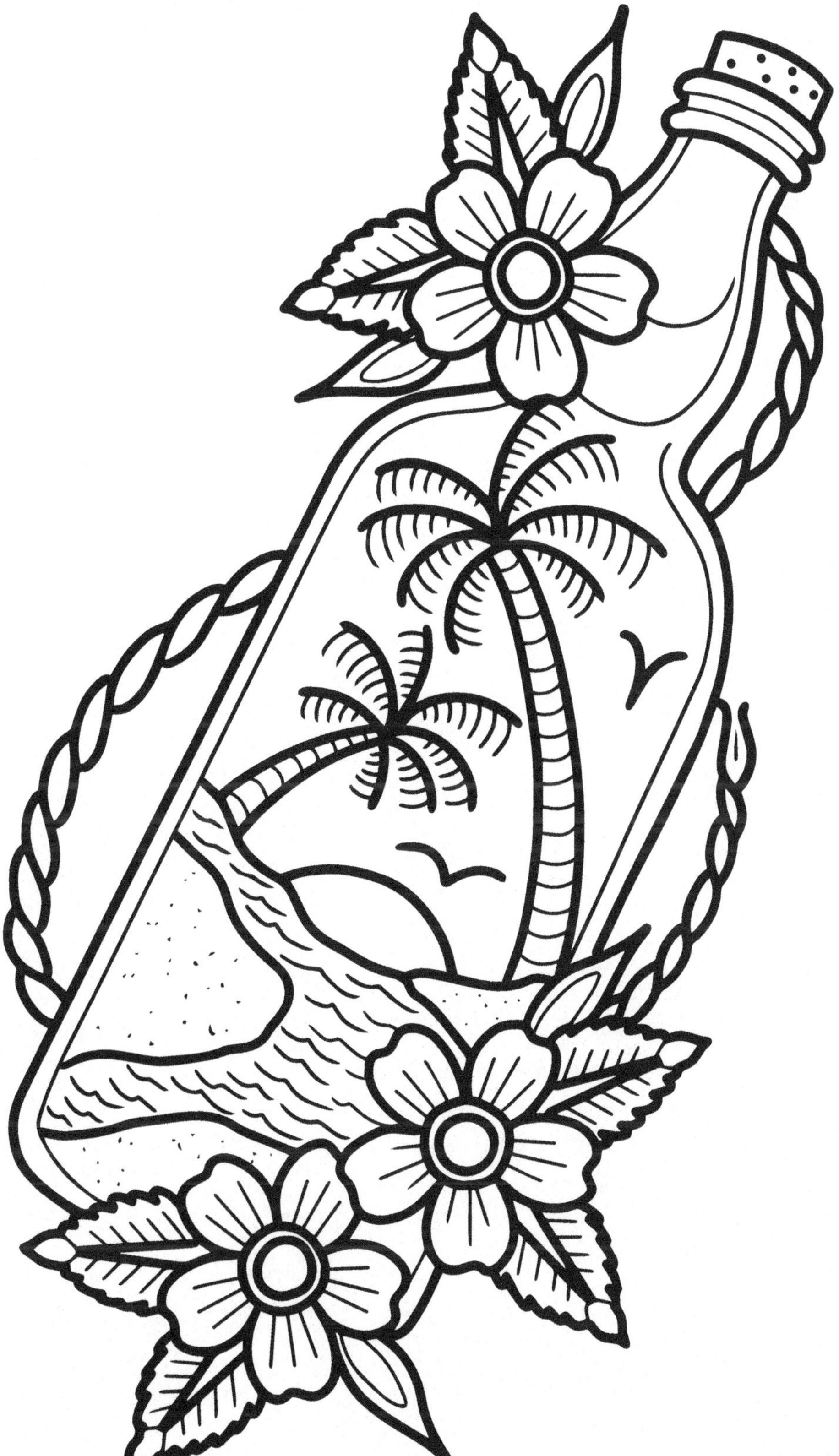

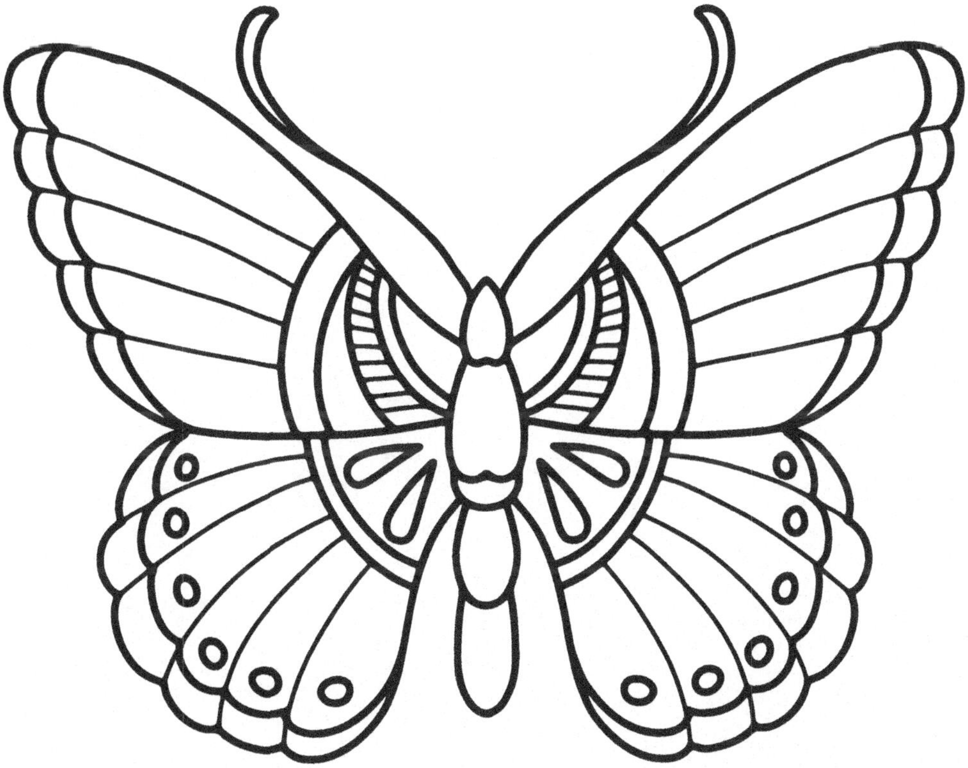

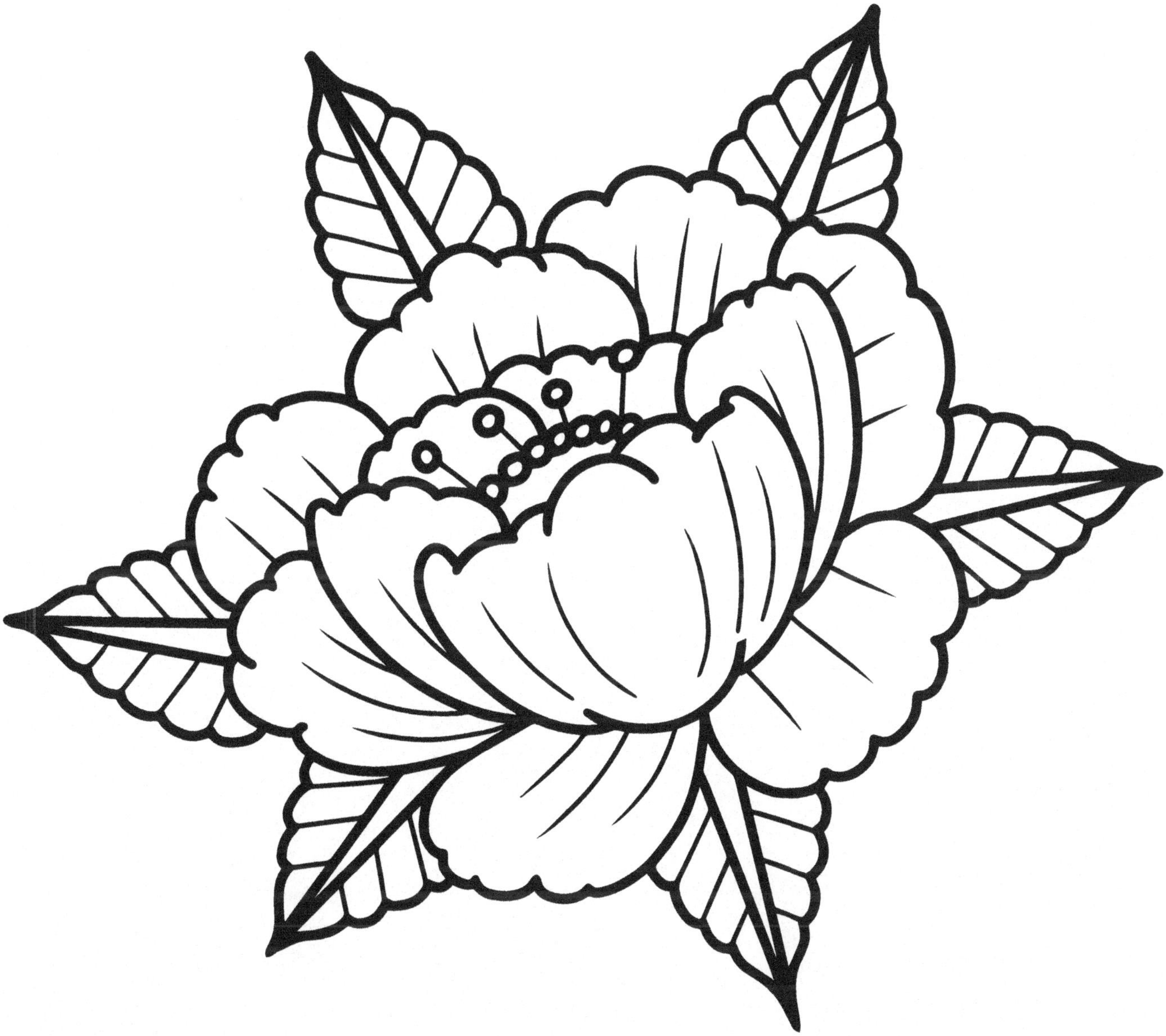

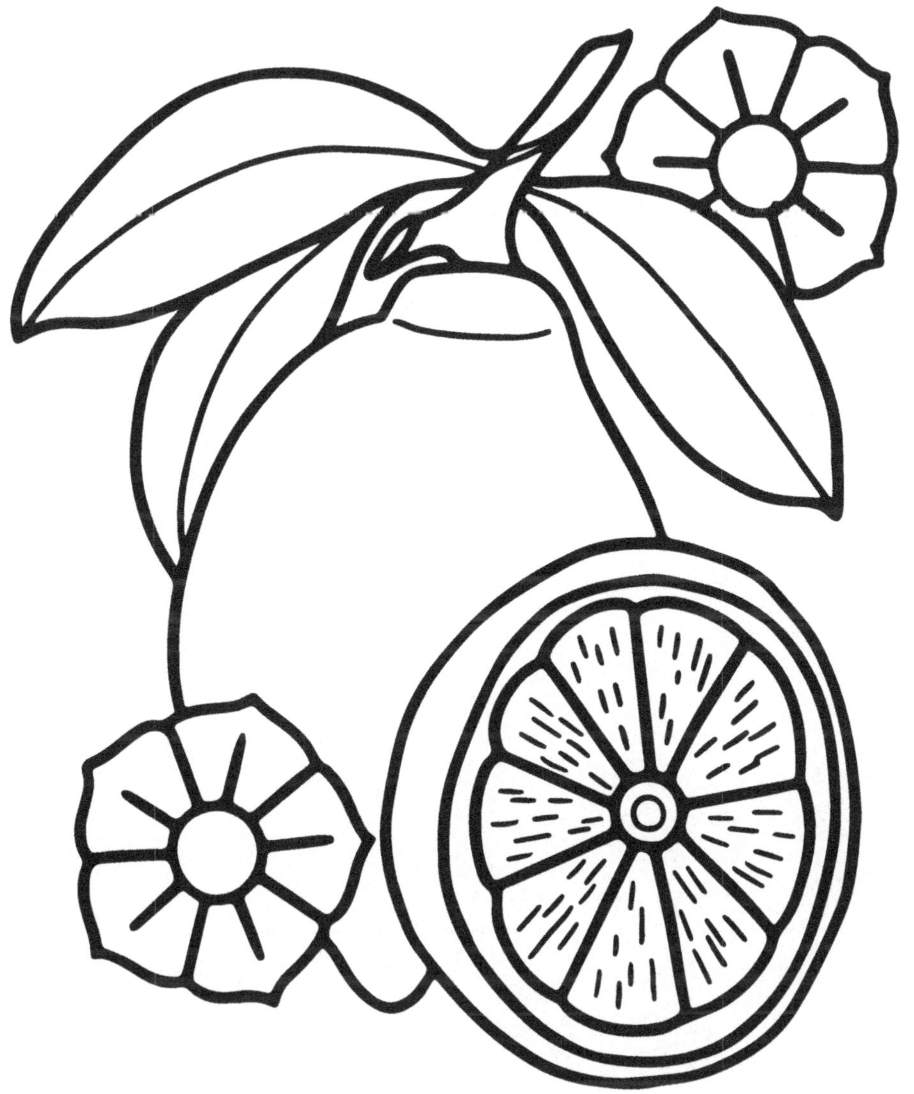

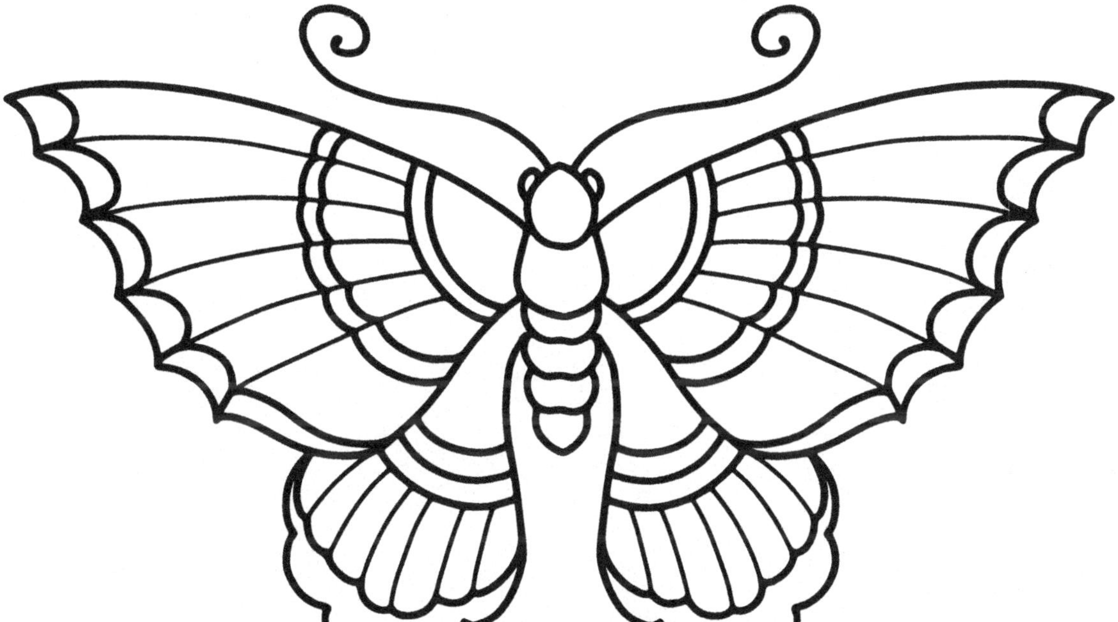

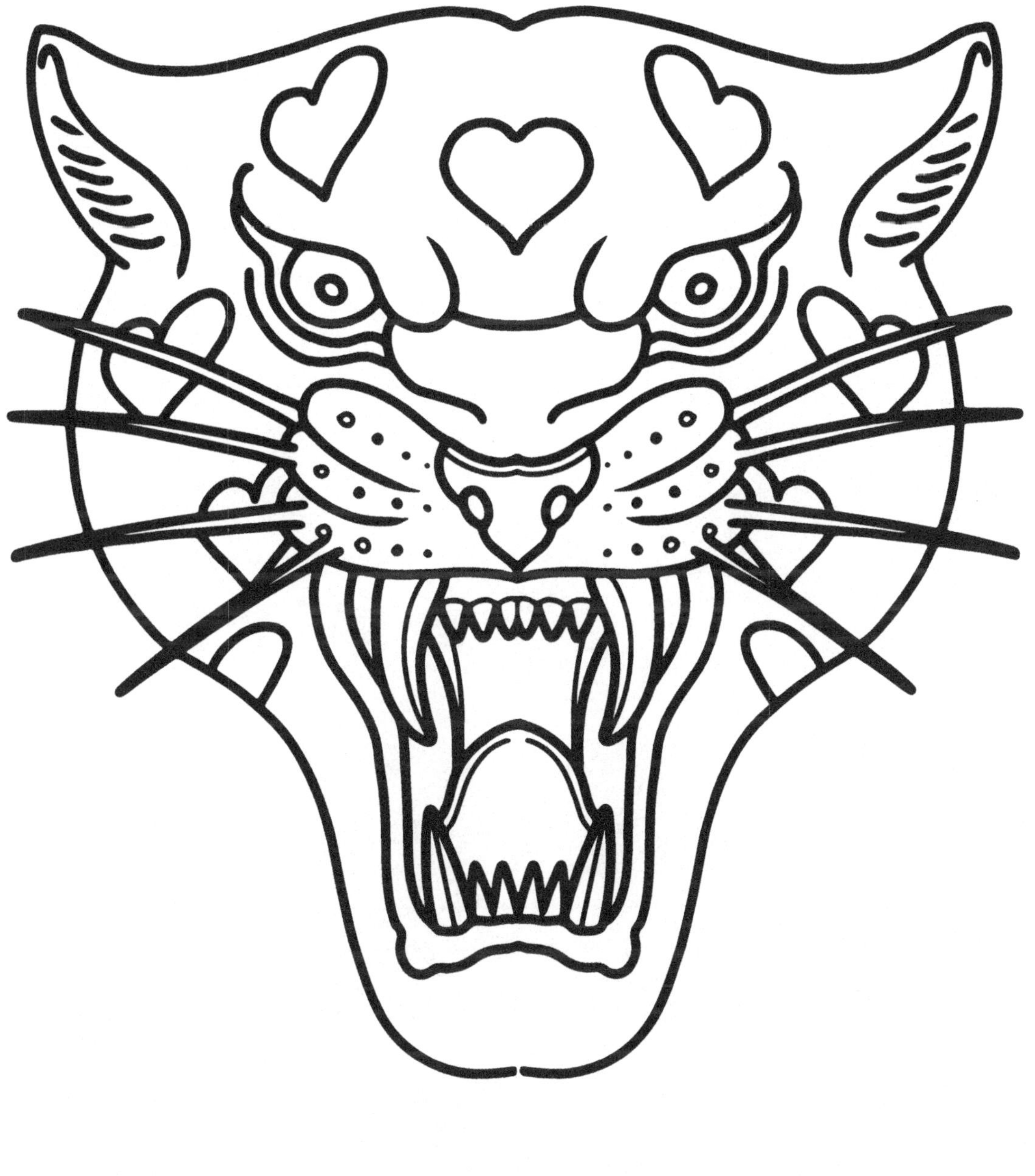

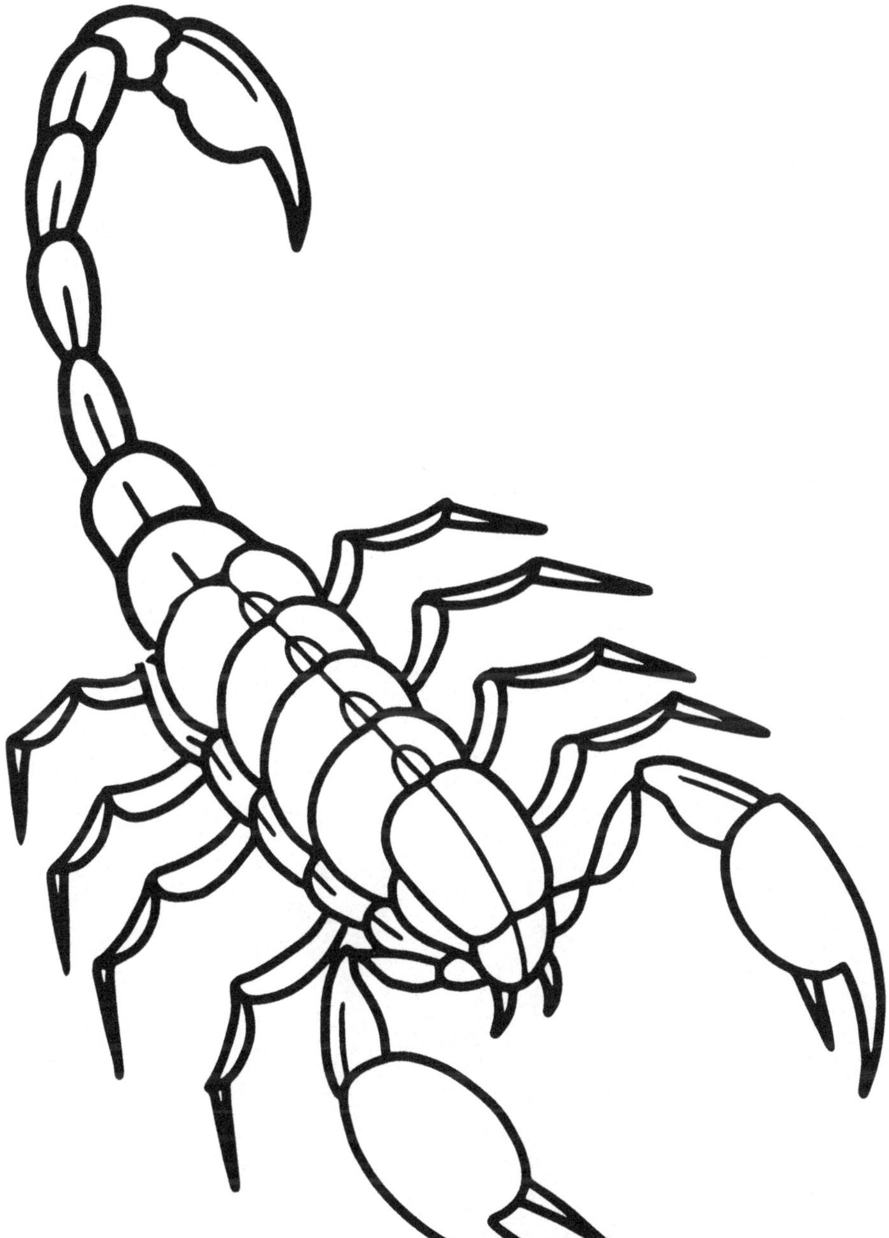

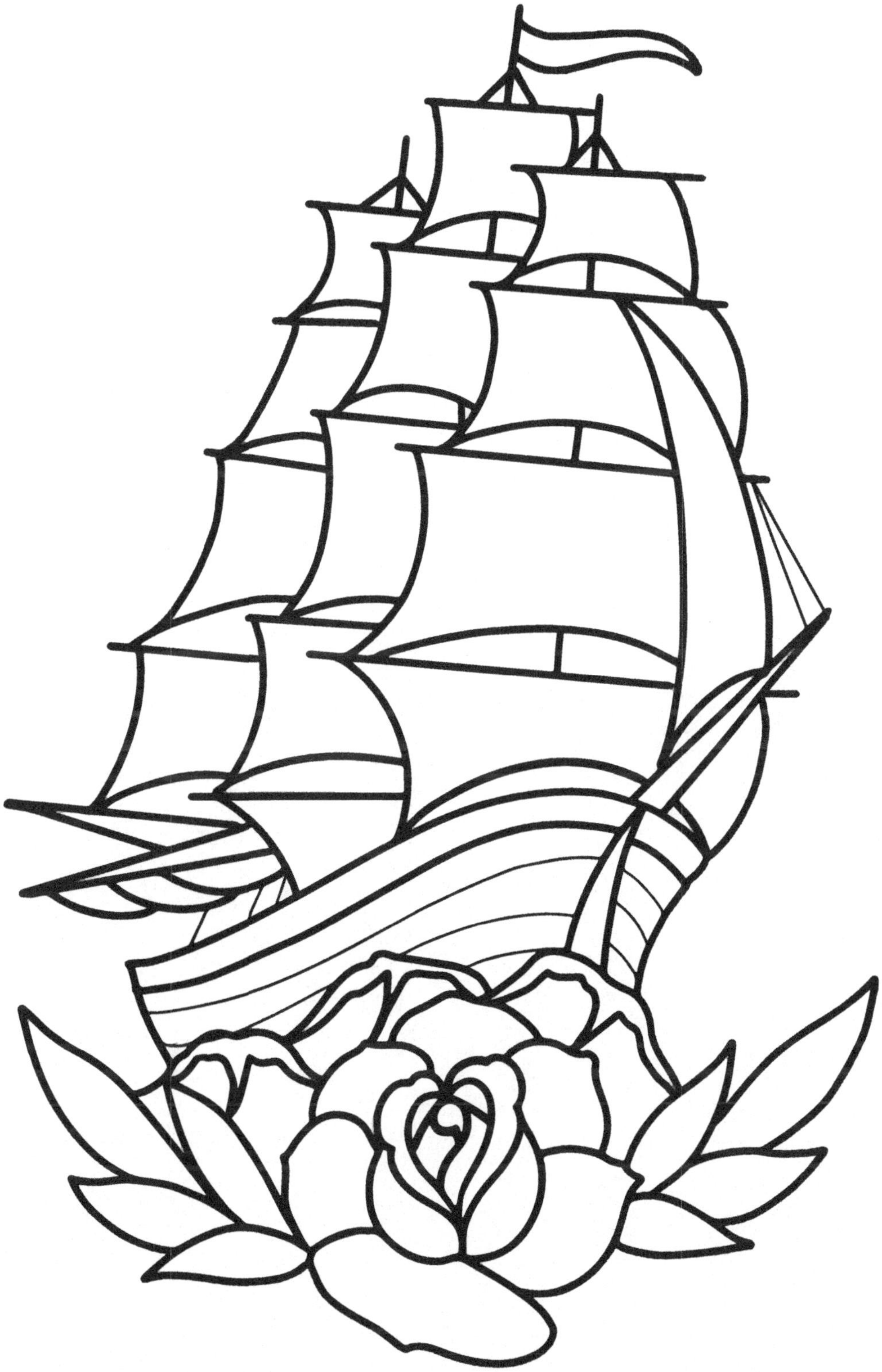

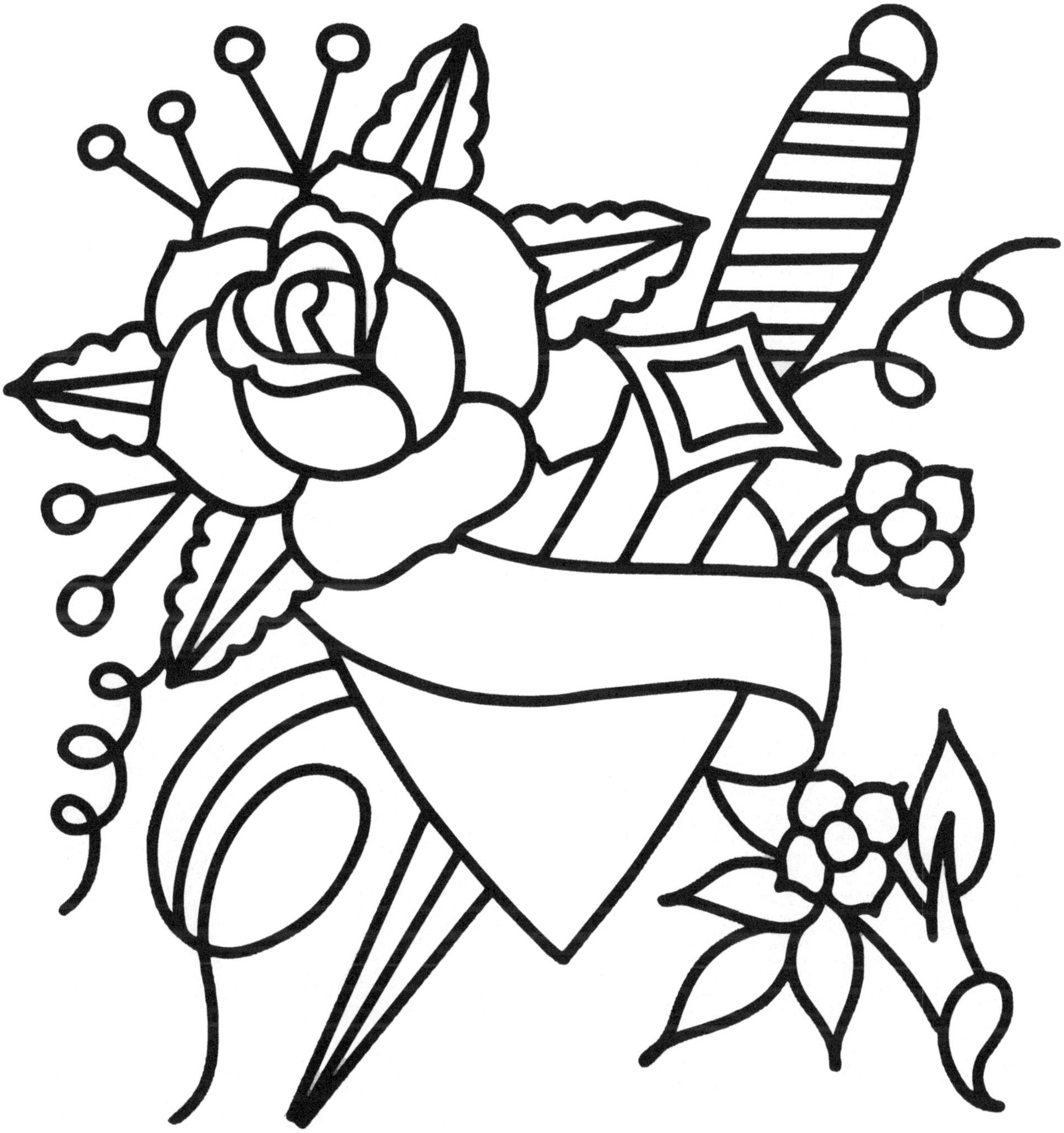

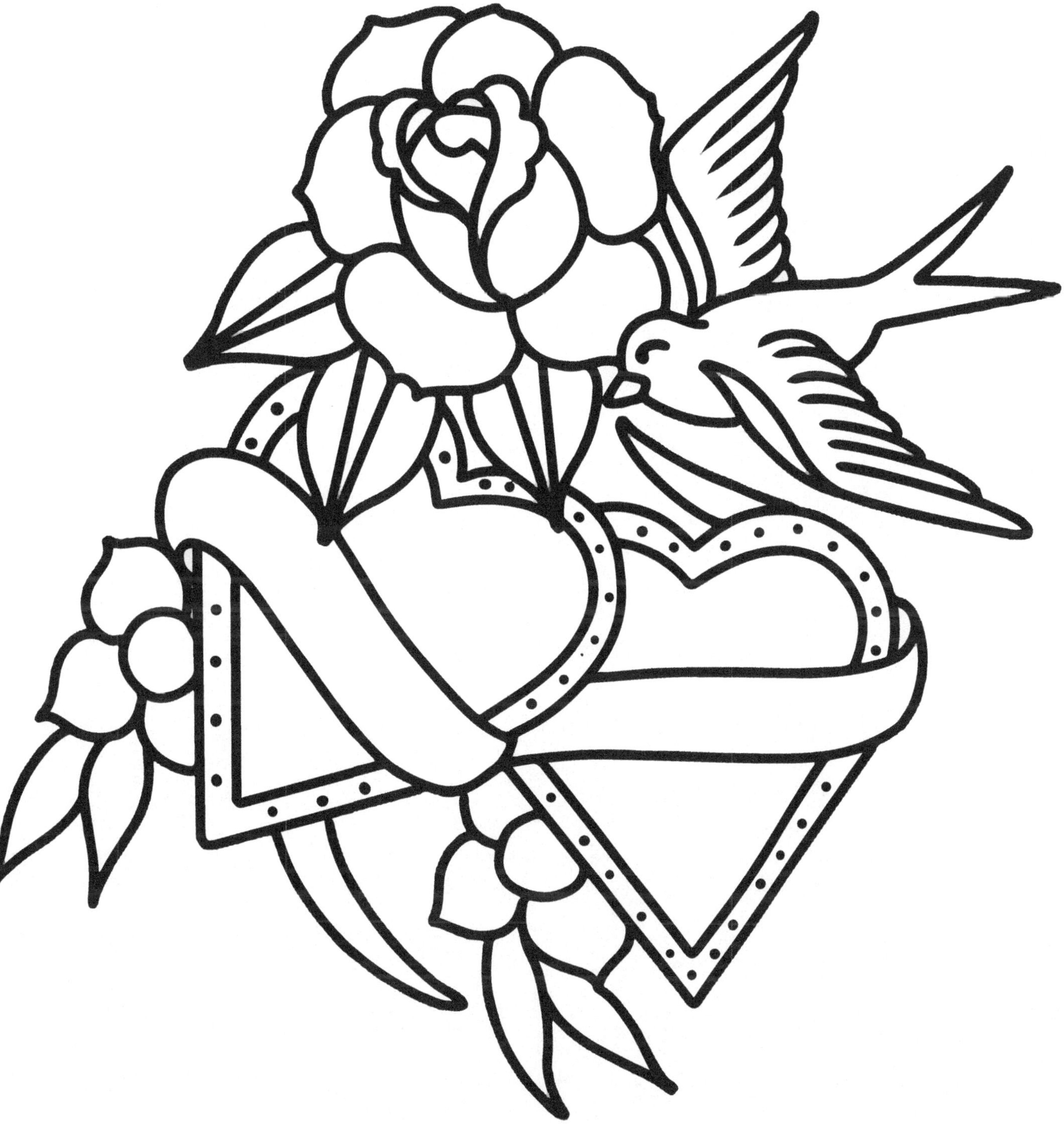

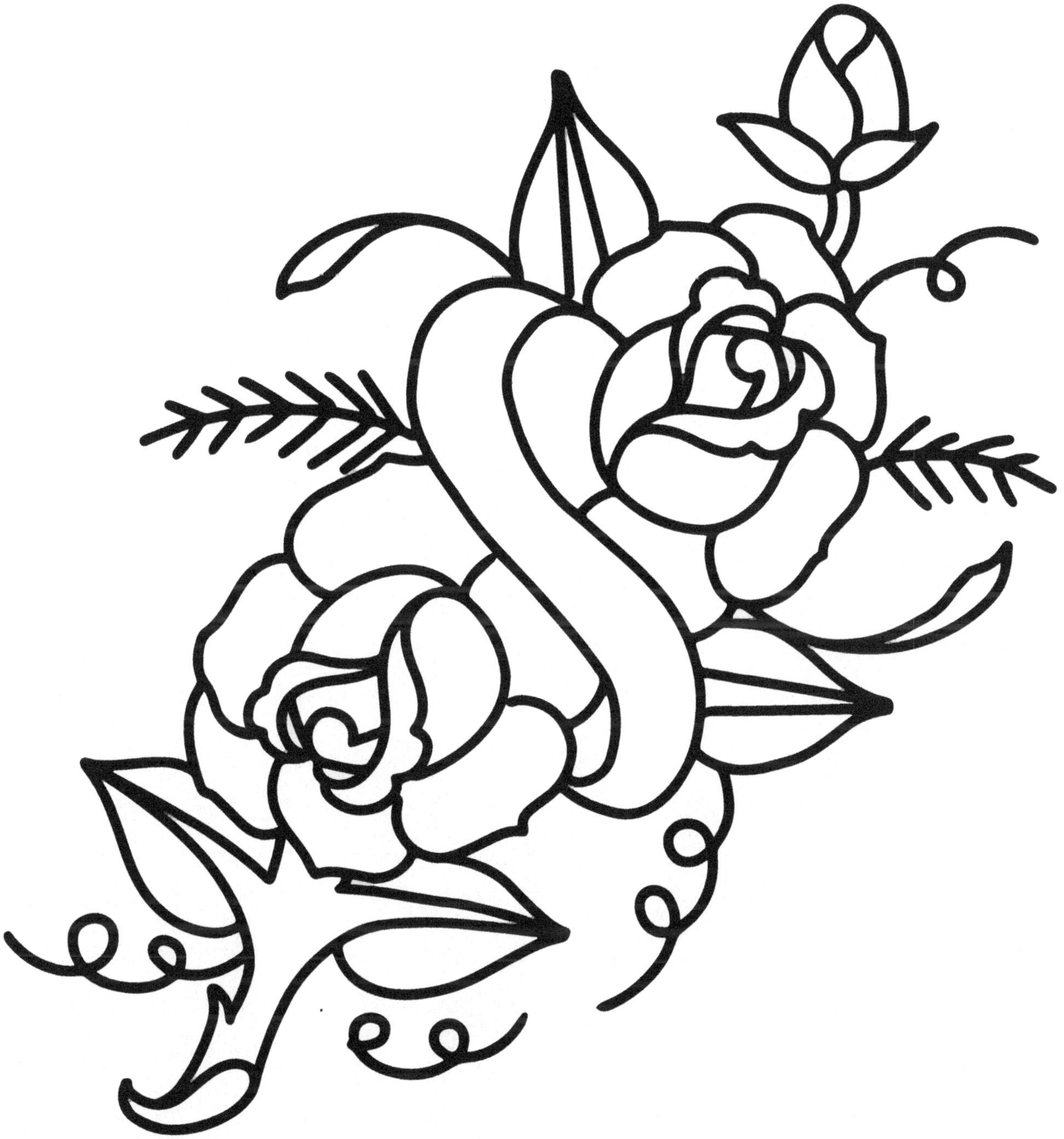

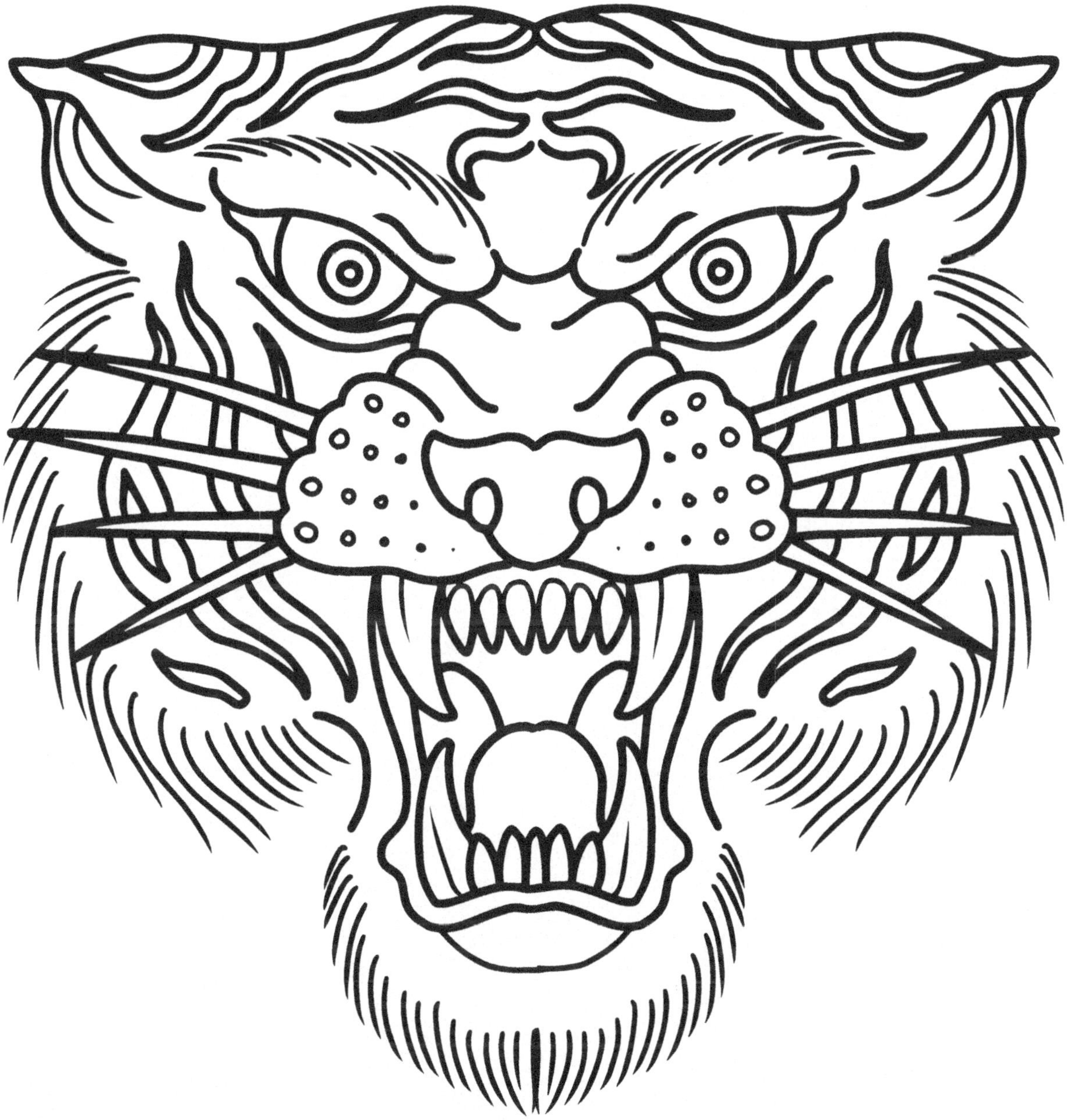

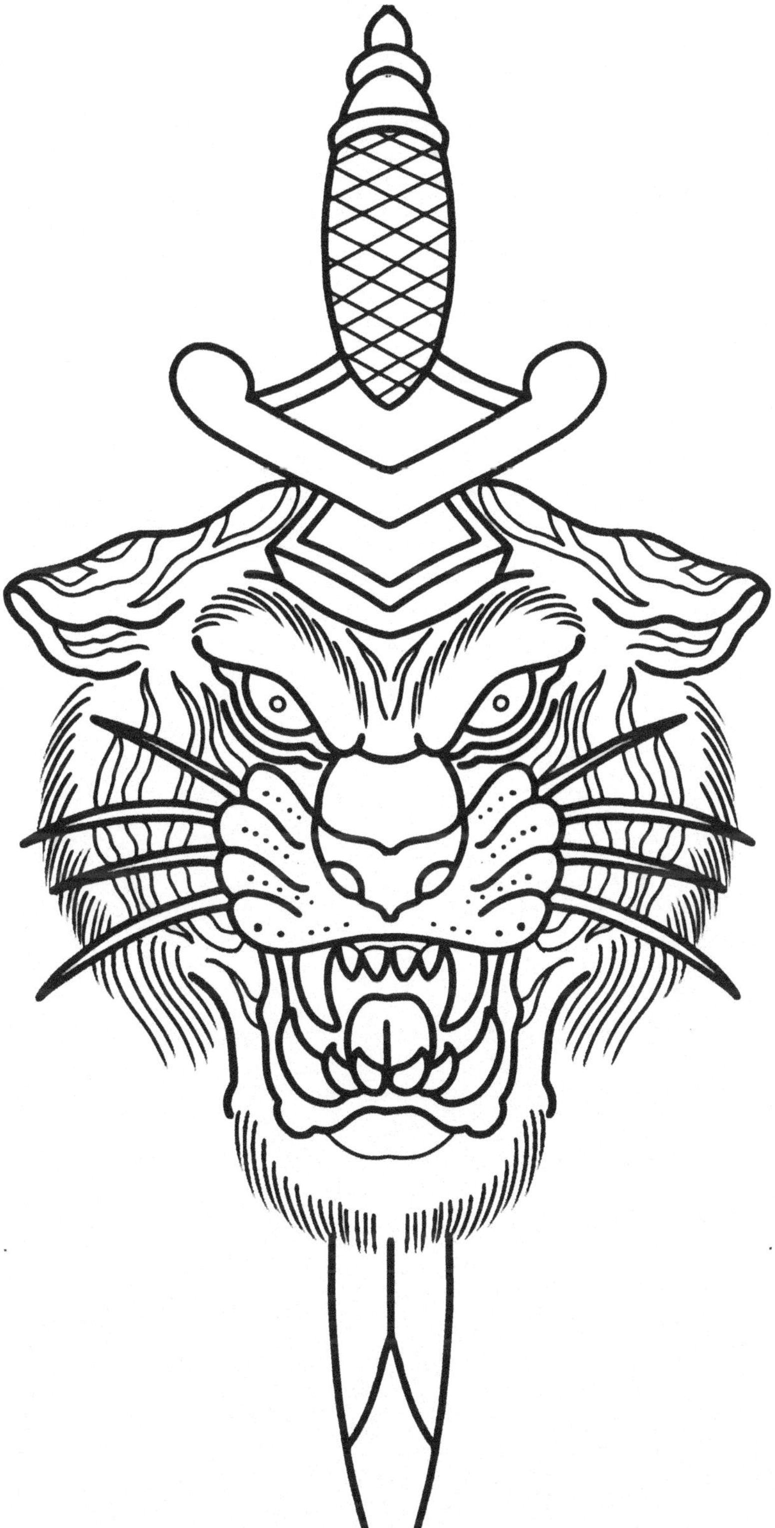

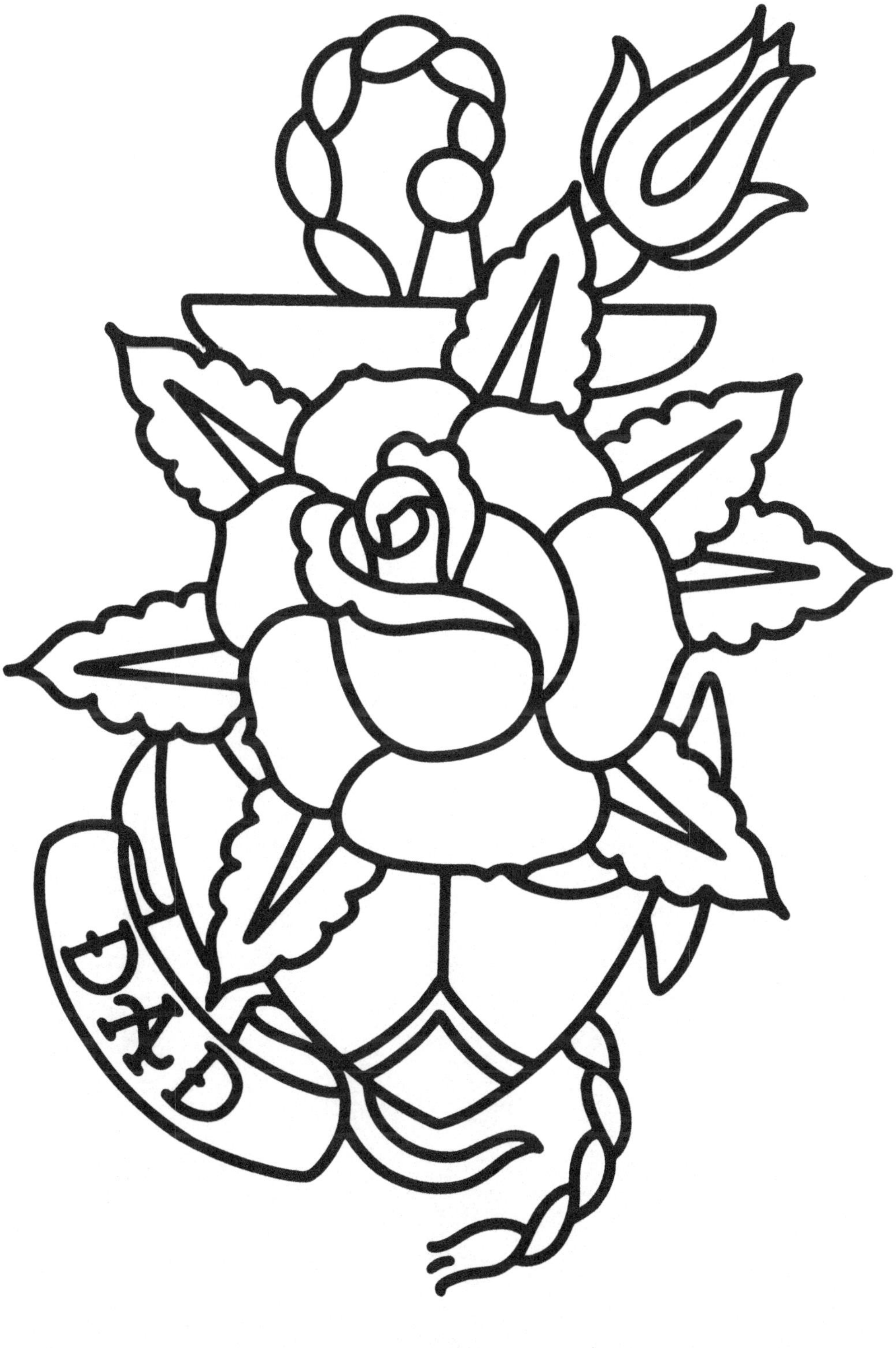
DAD

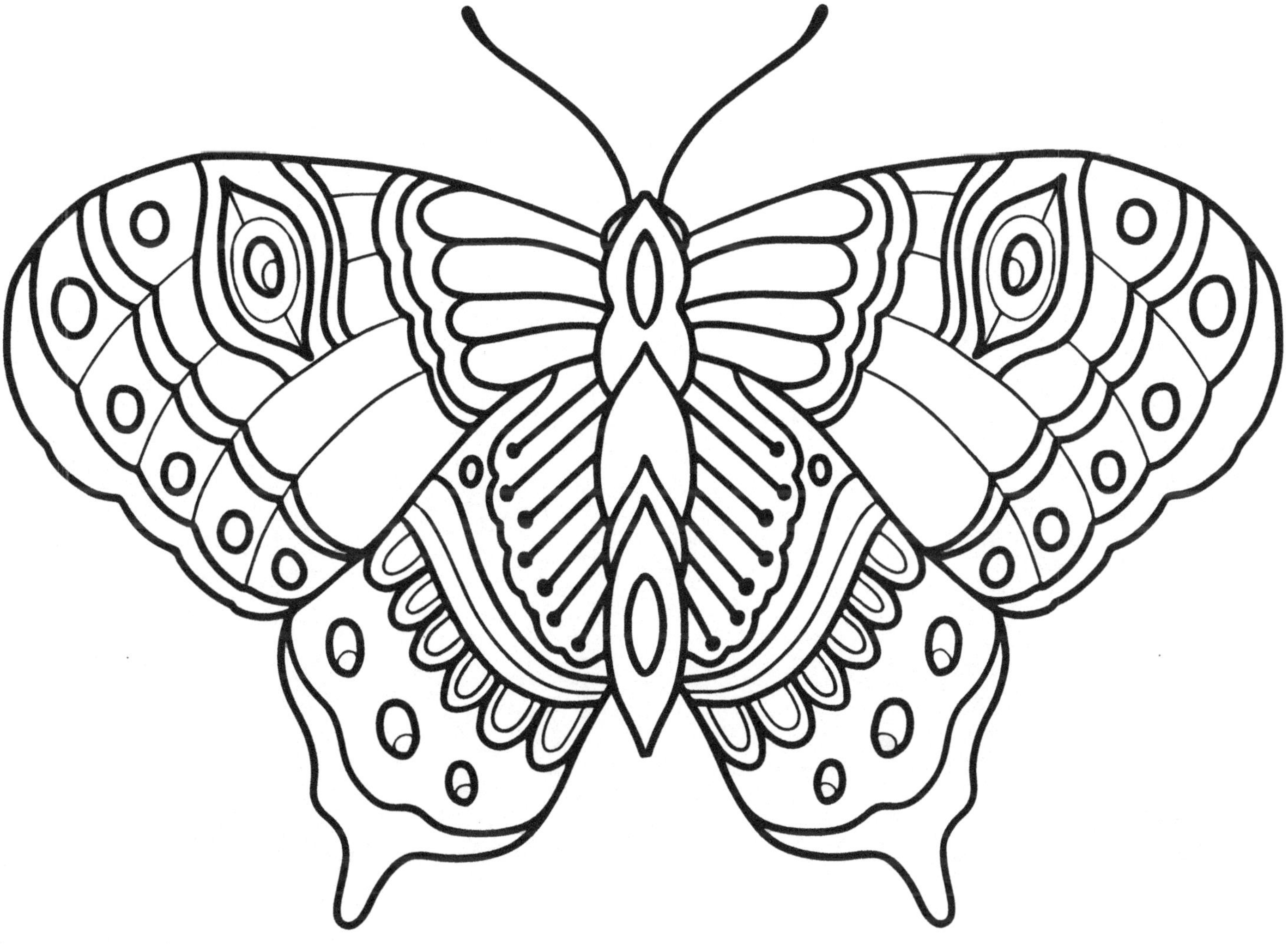

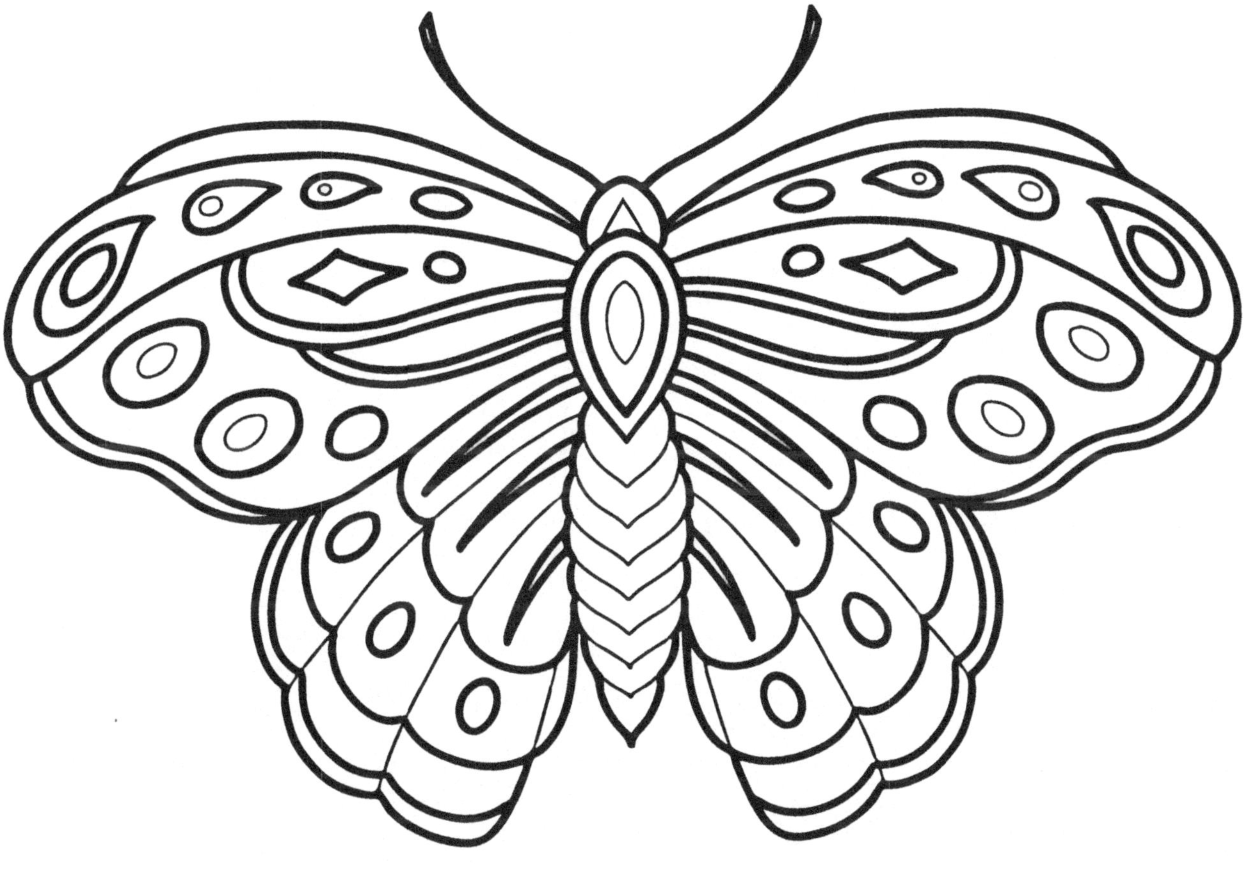

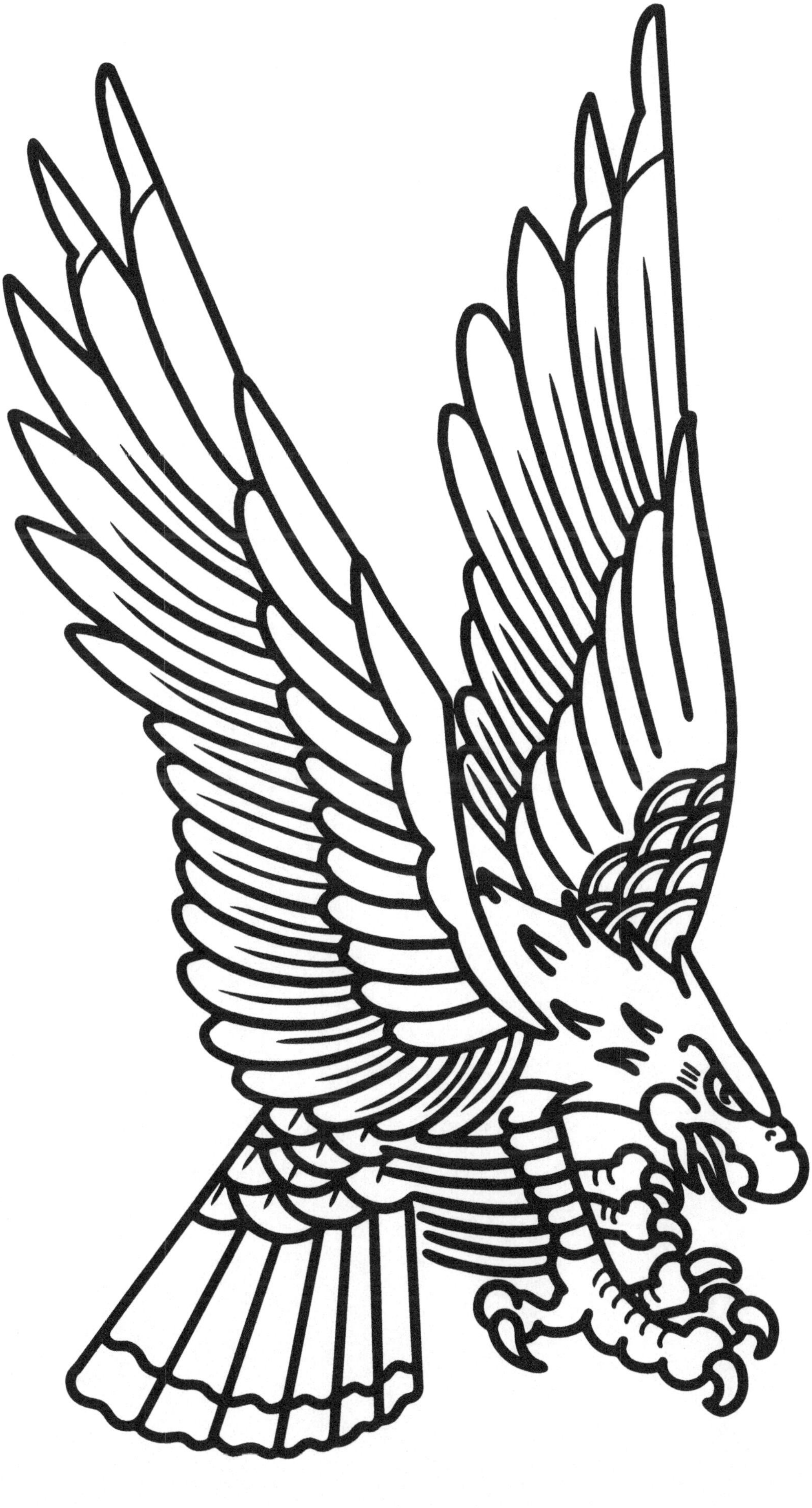

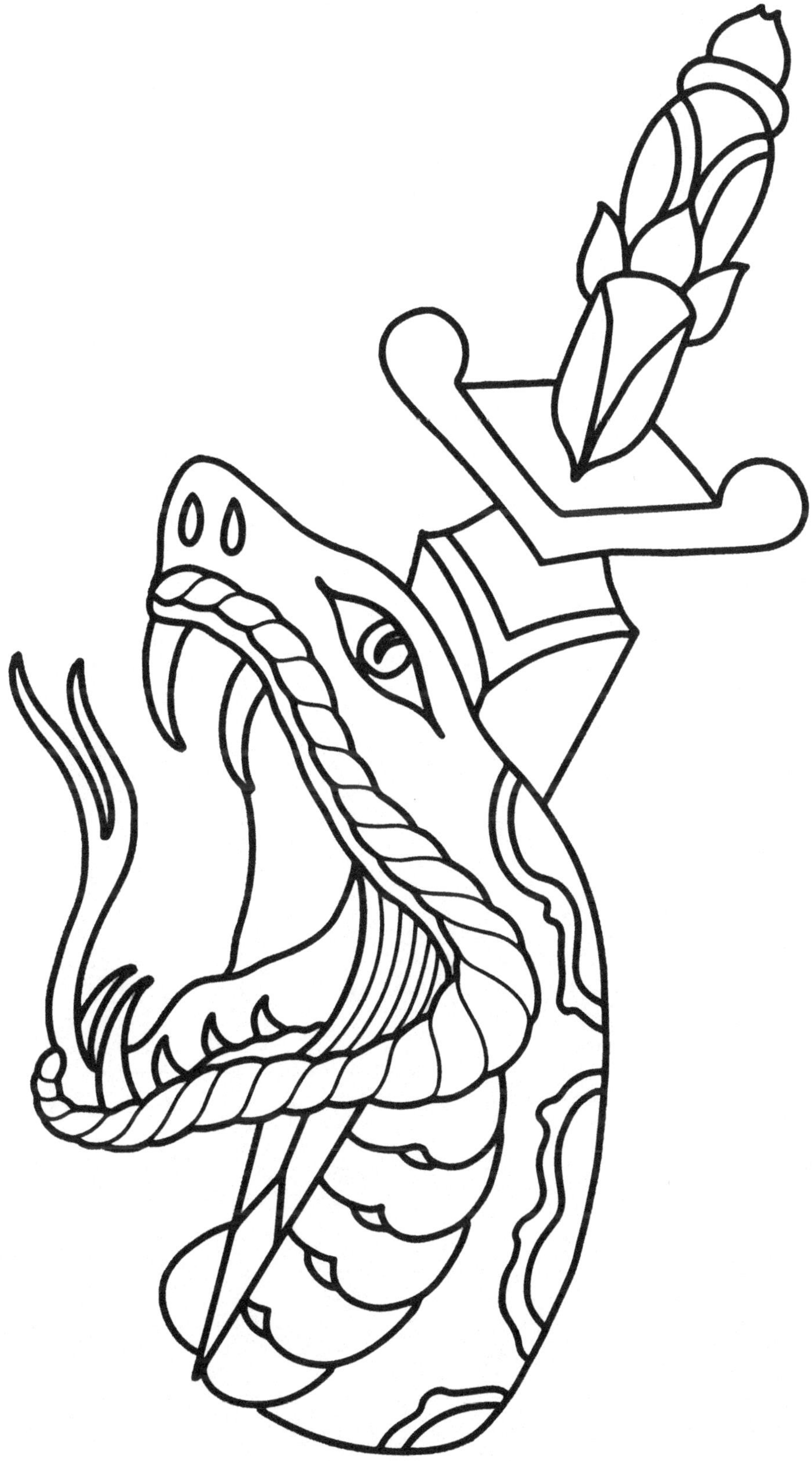

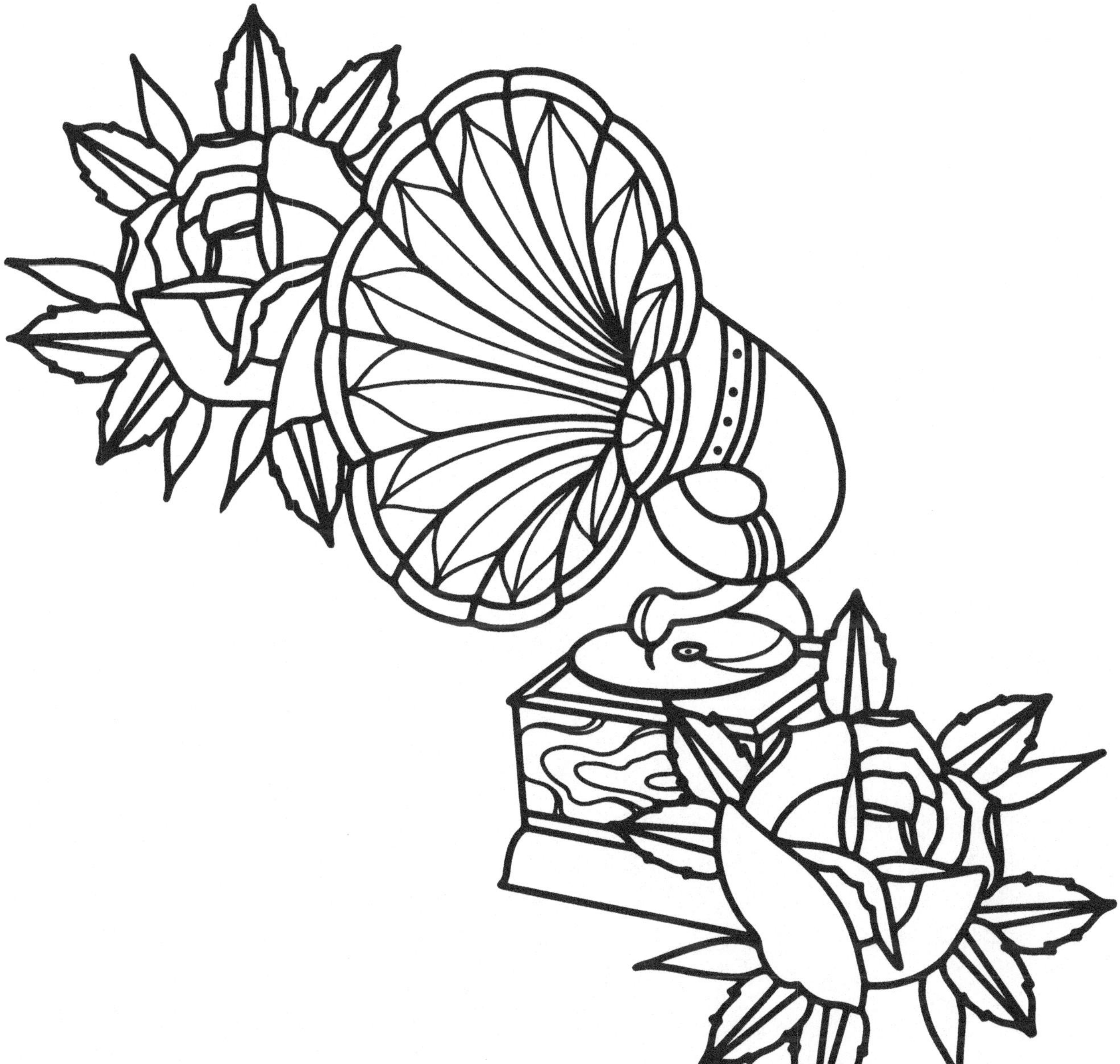

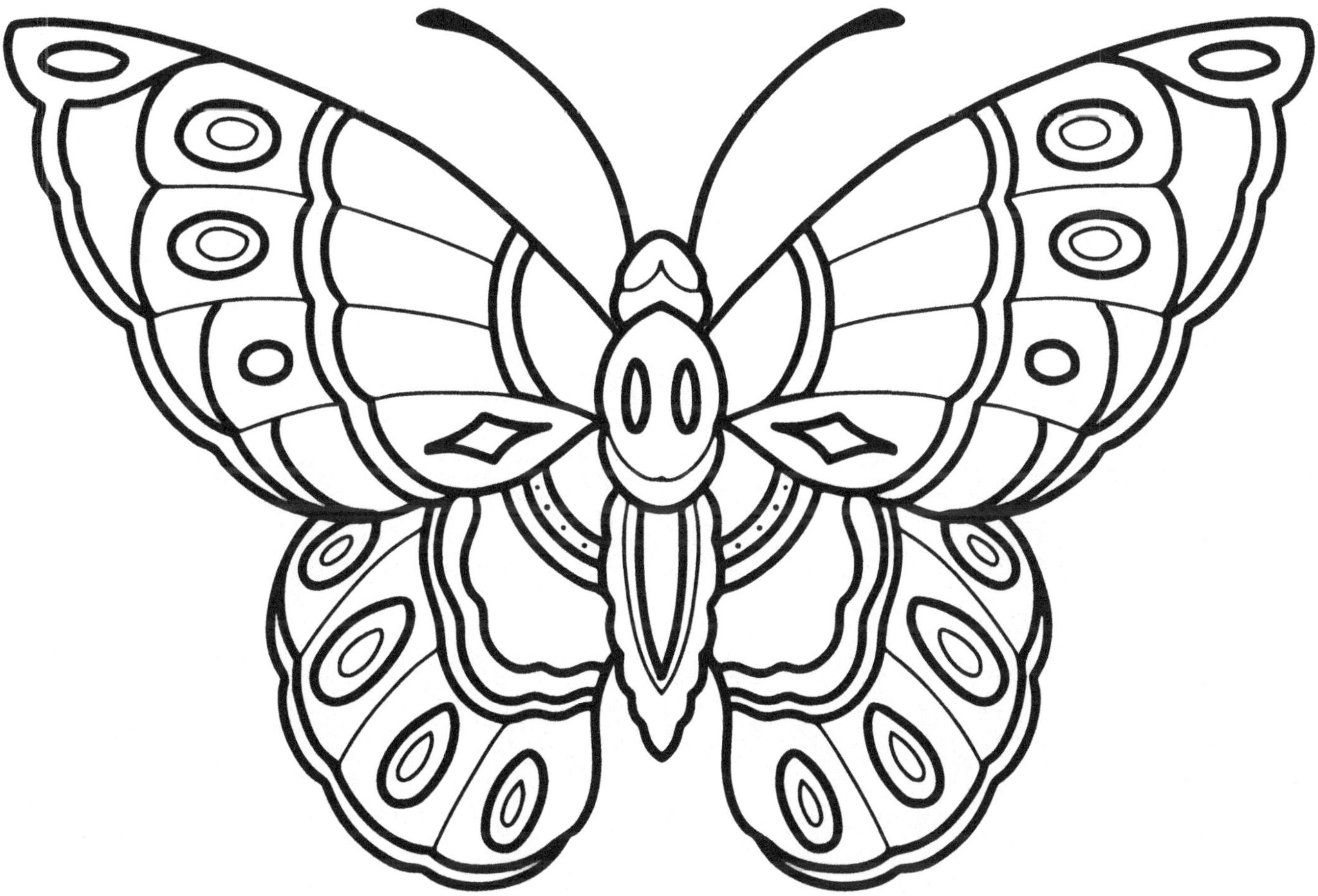

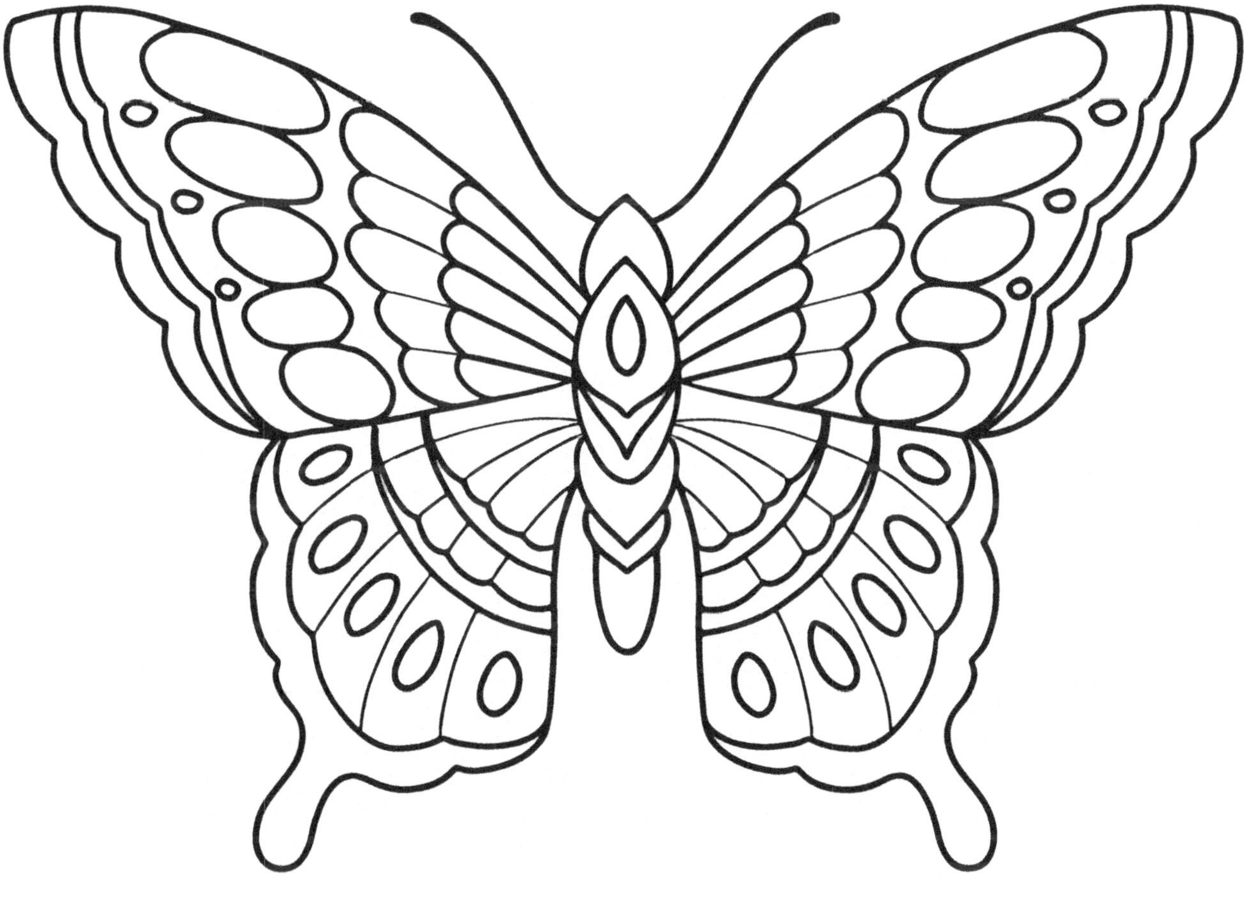

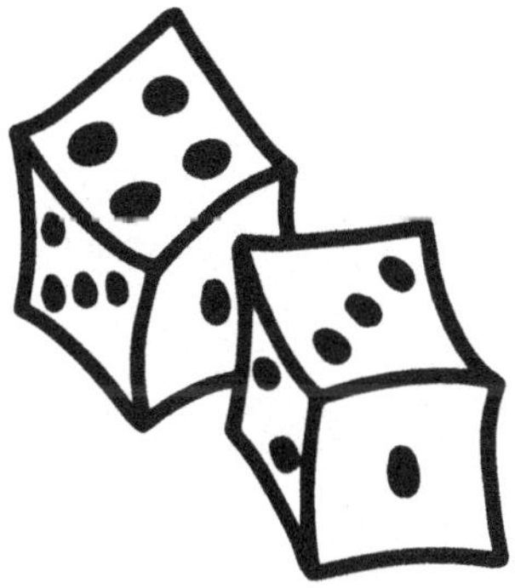
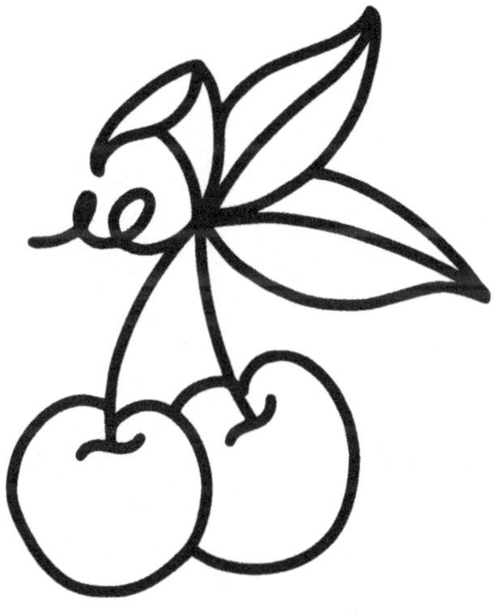
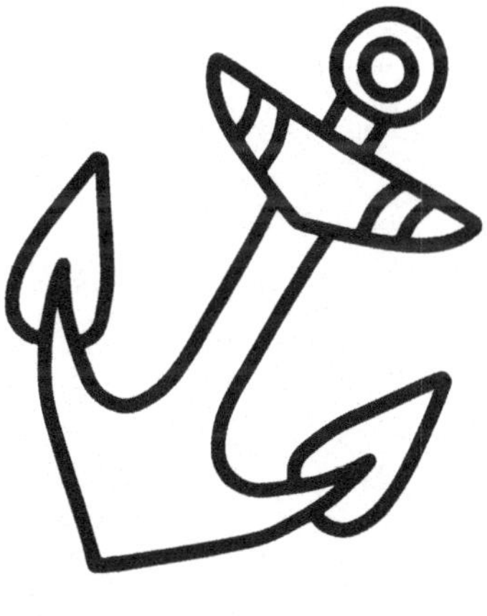

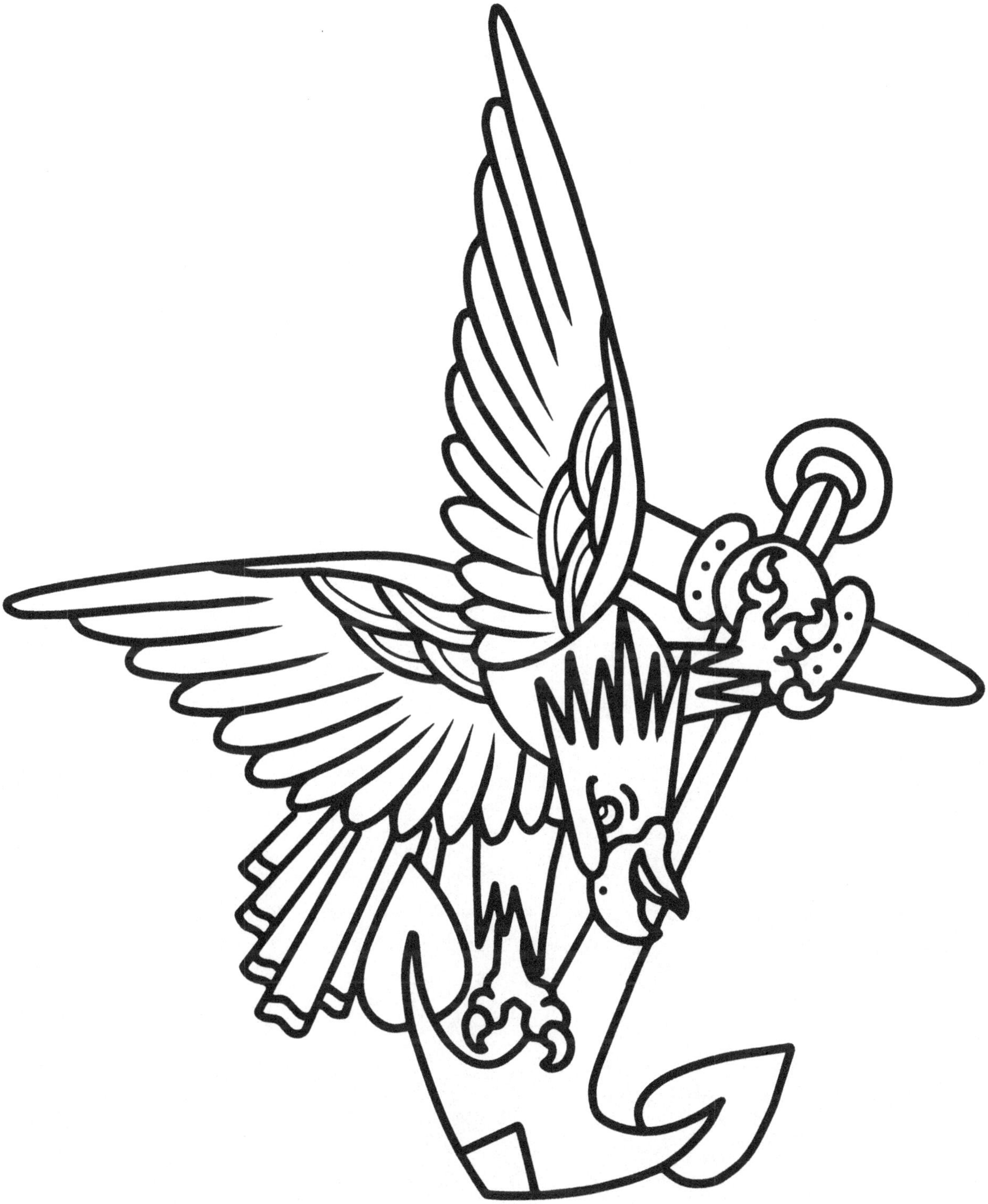

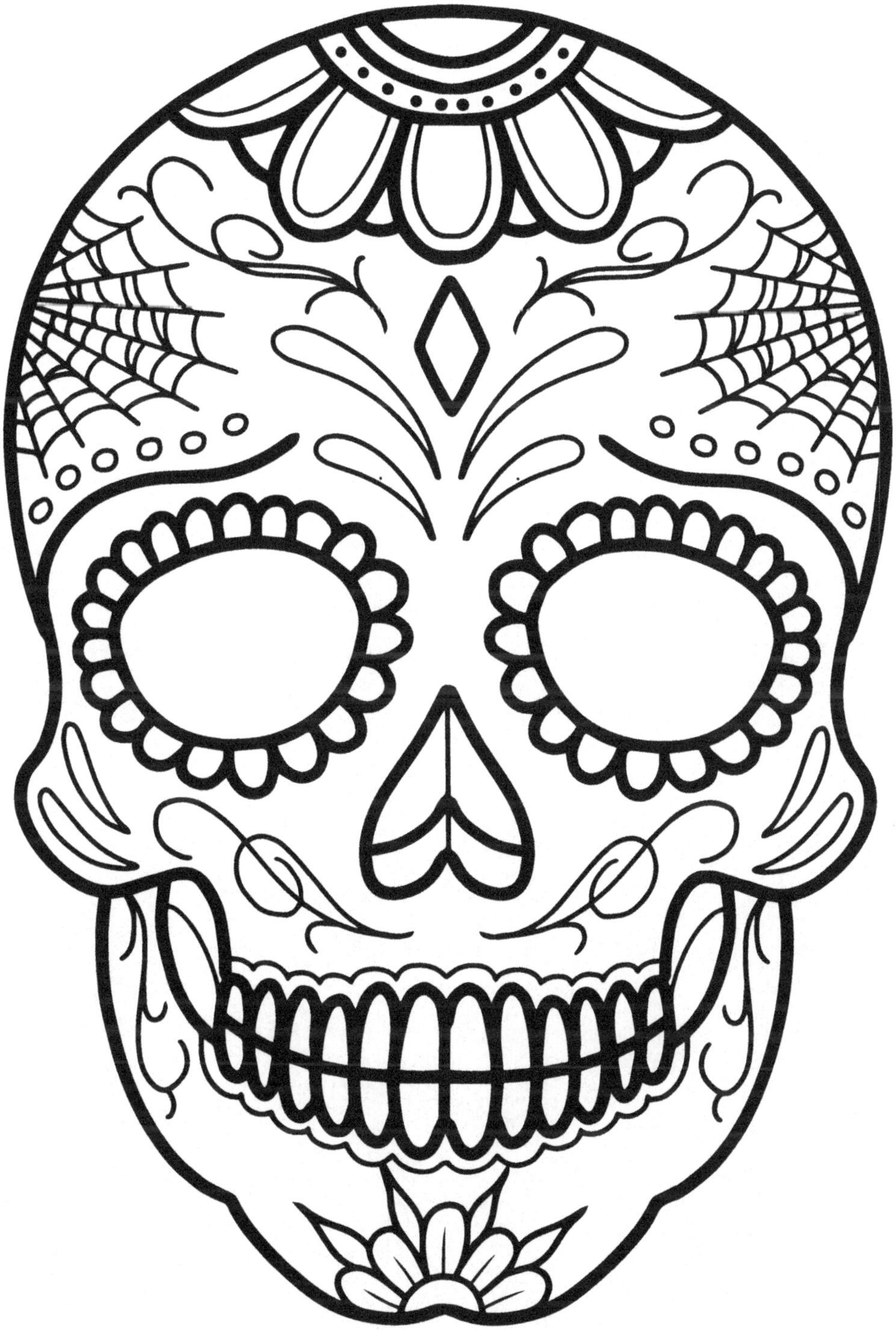

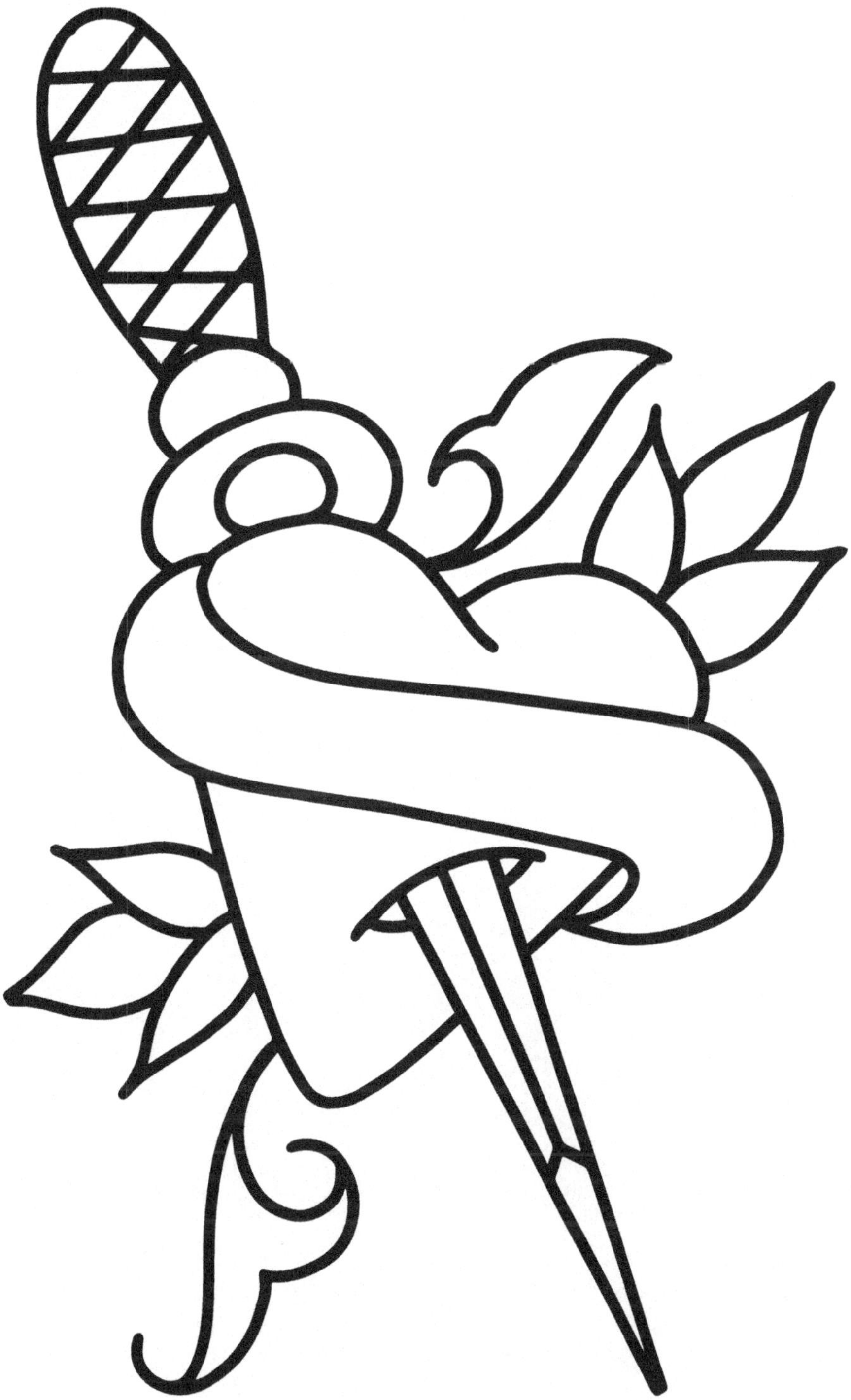

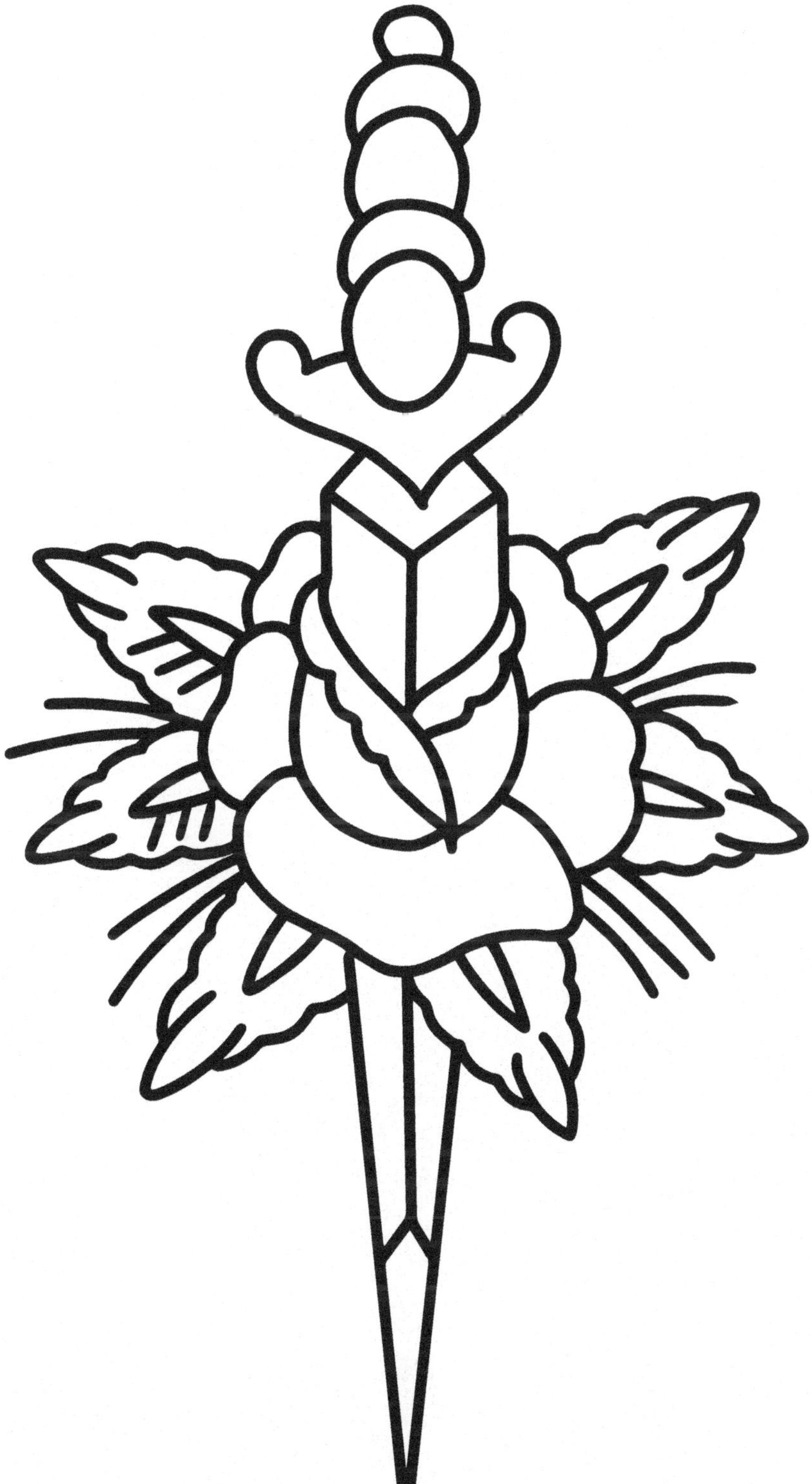

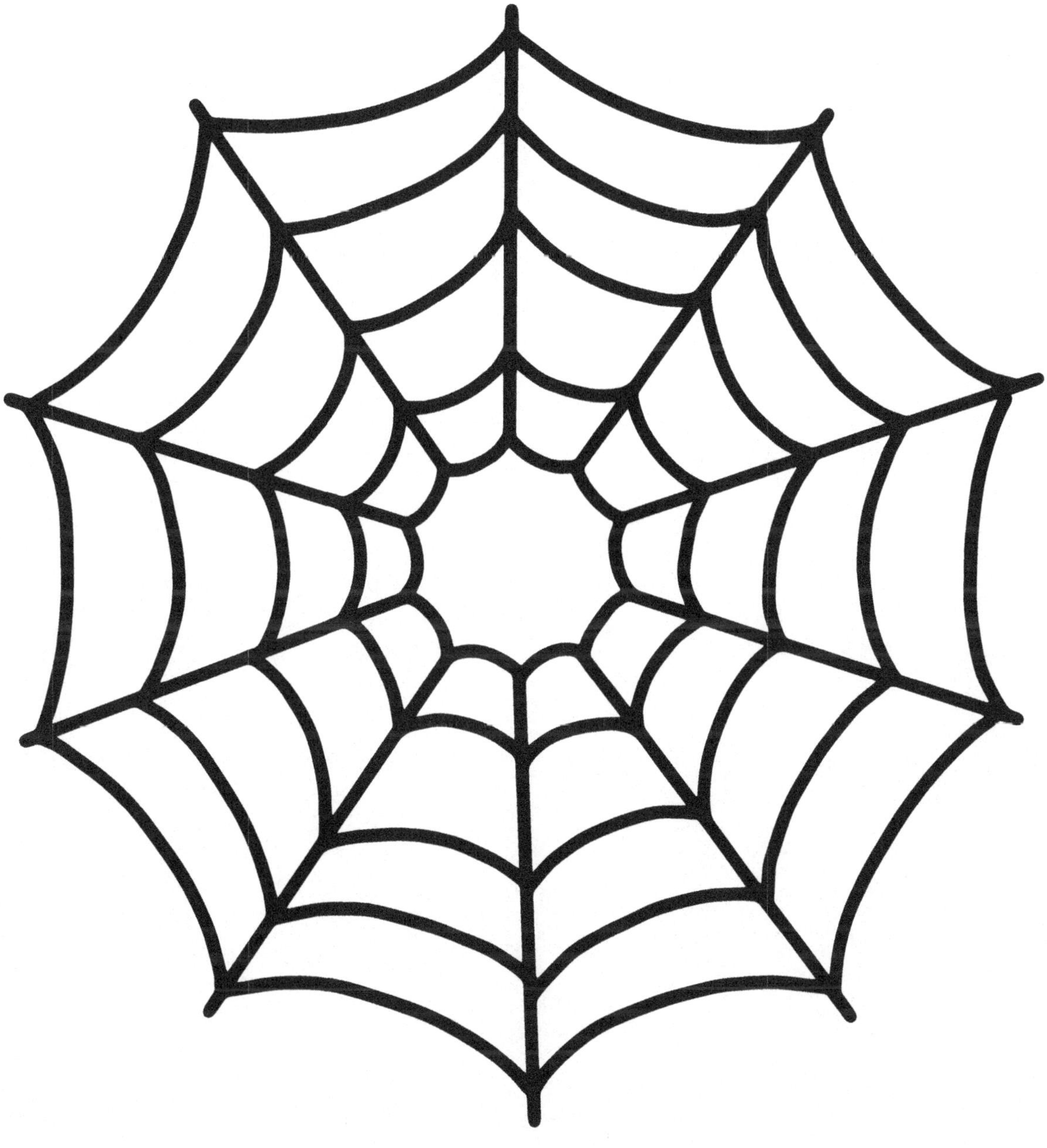

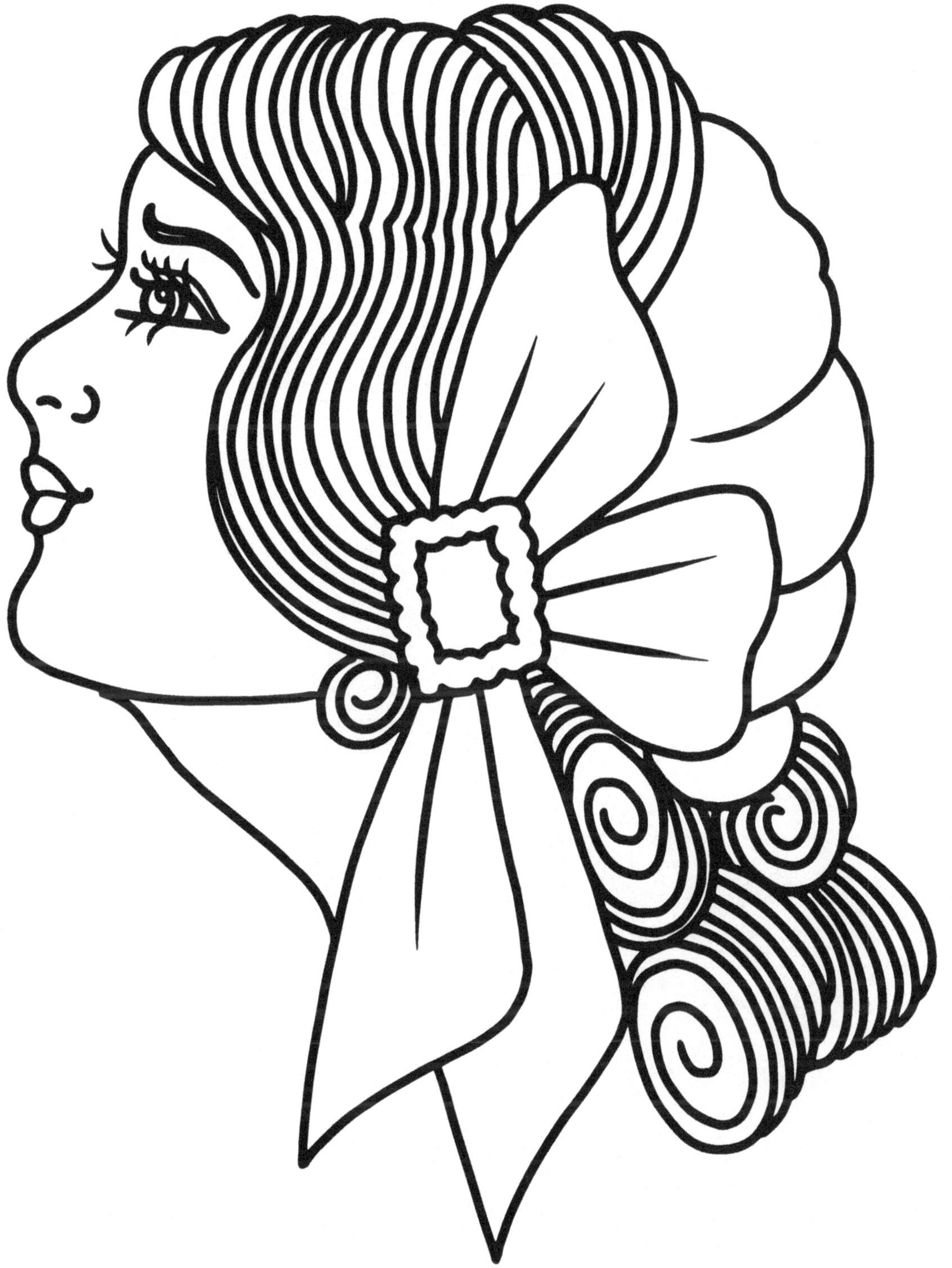

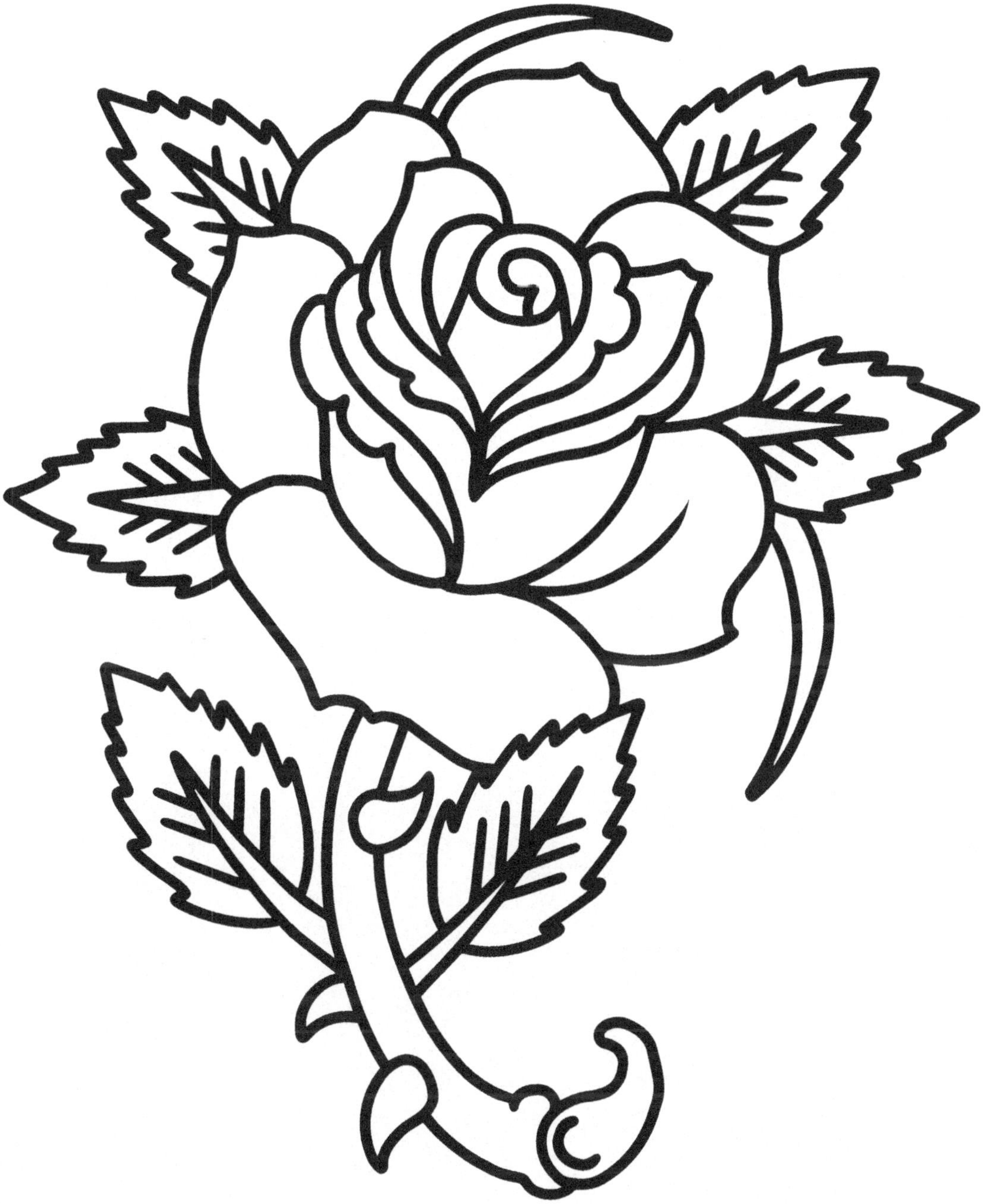

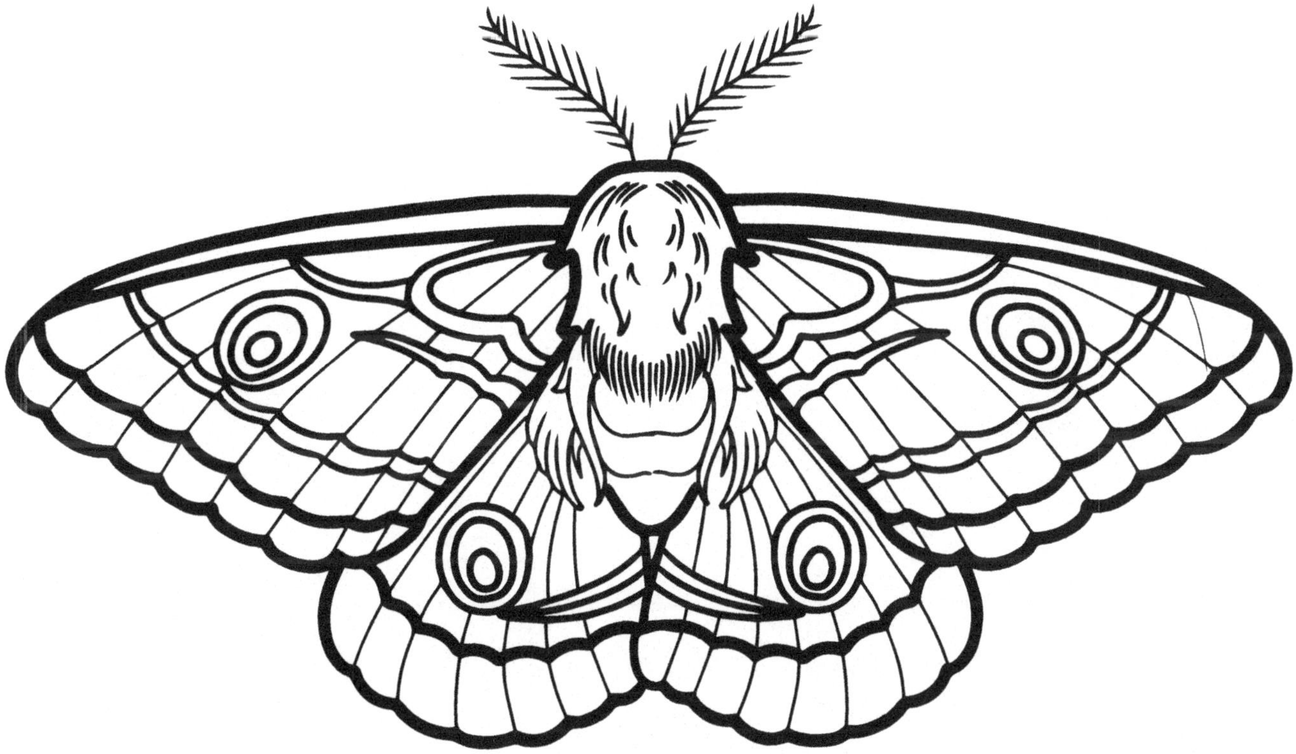

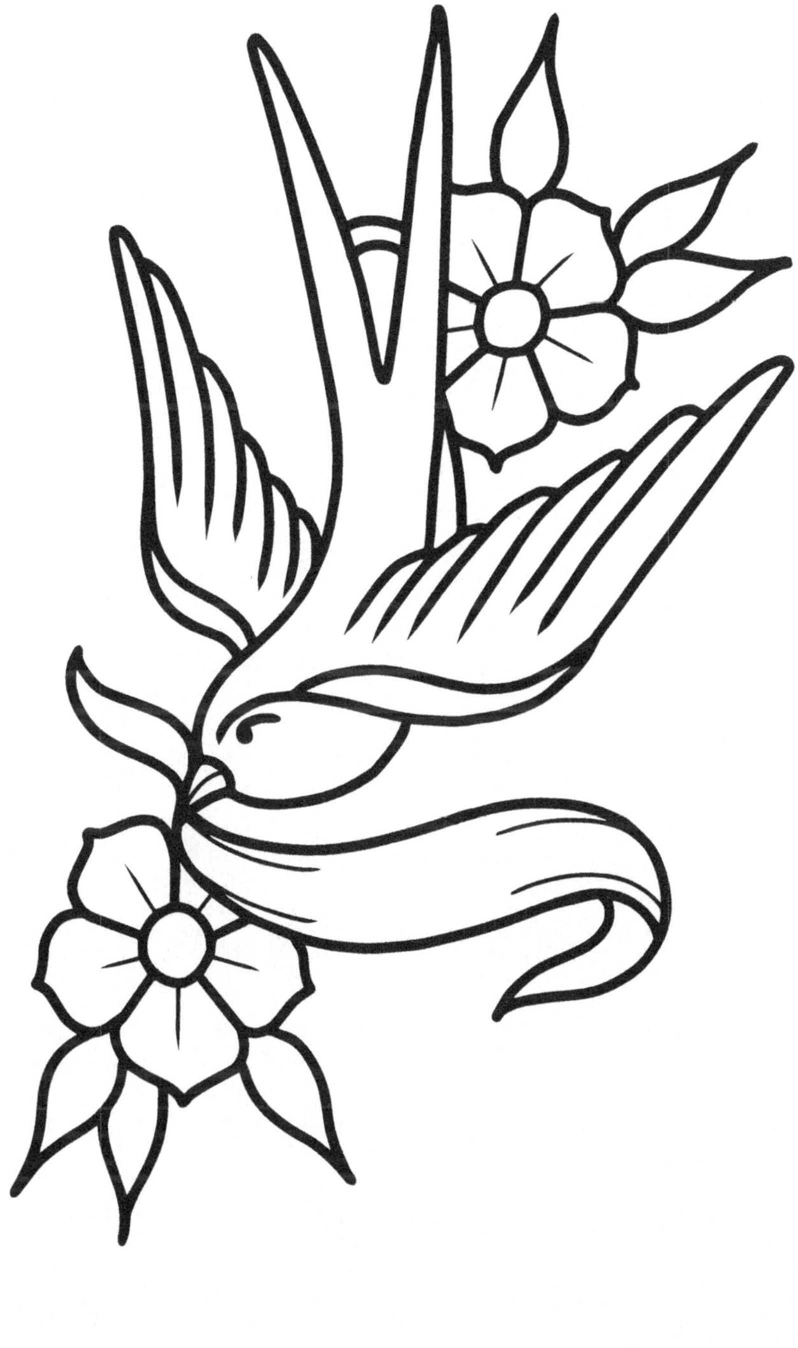

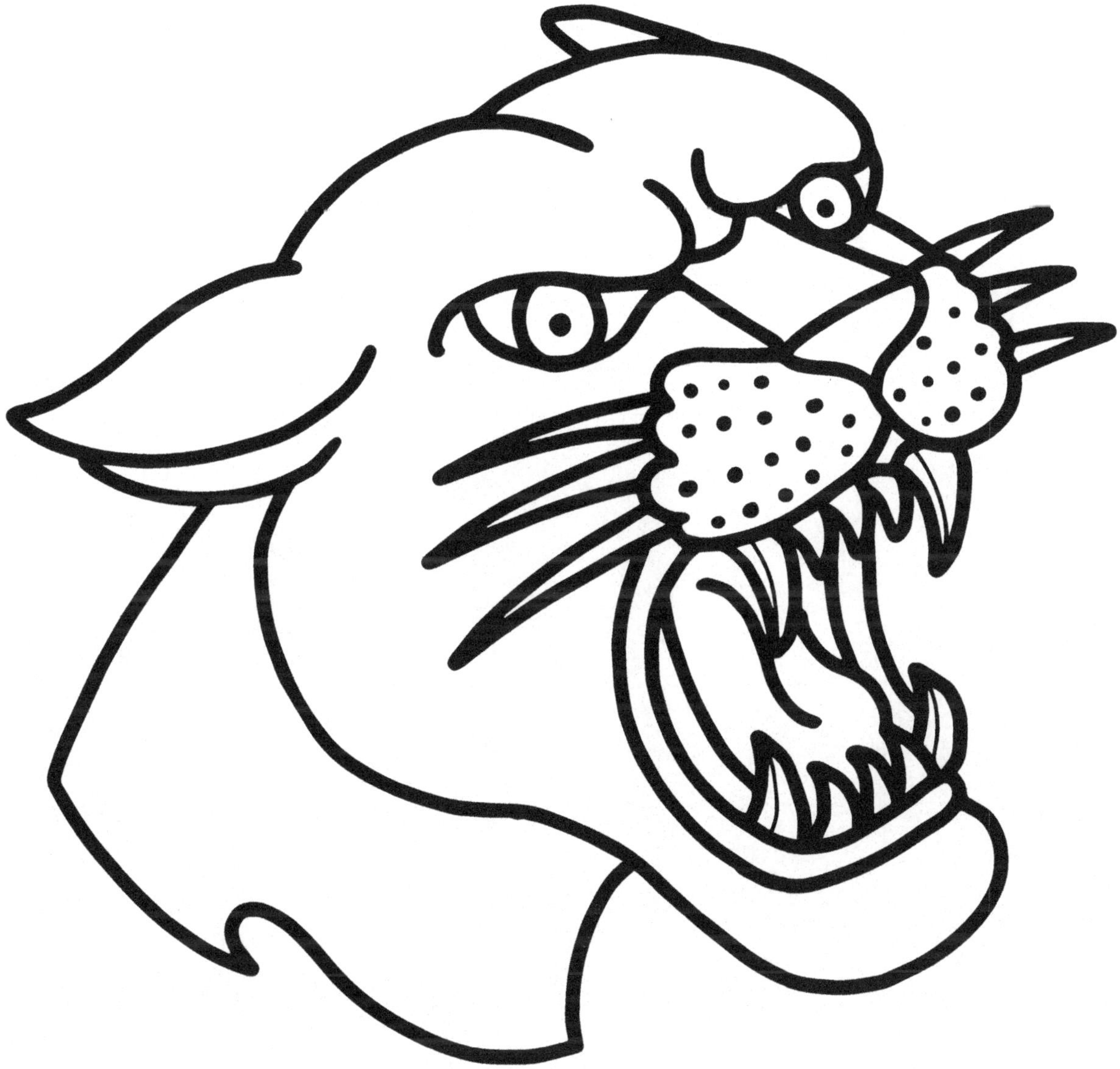

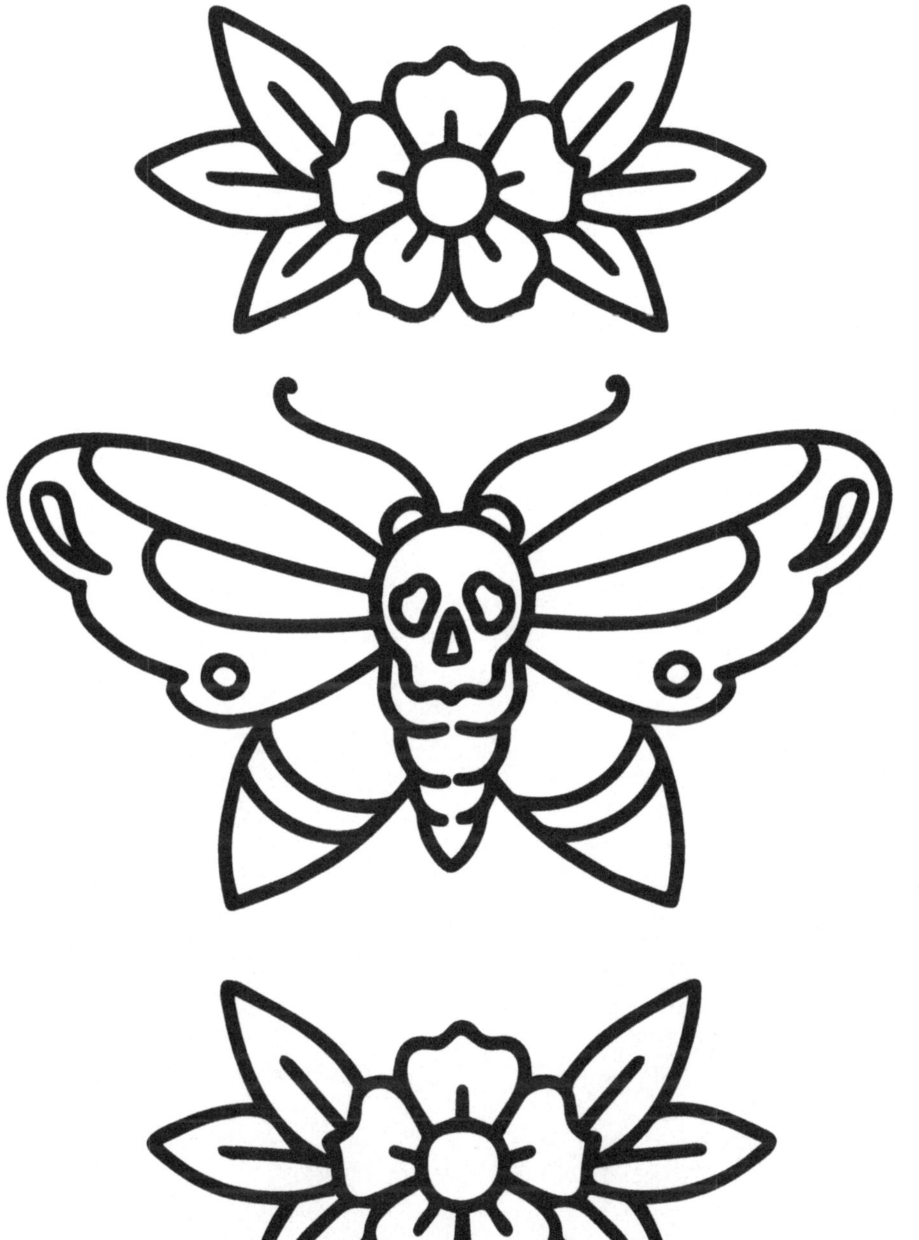

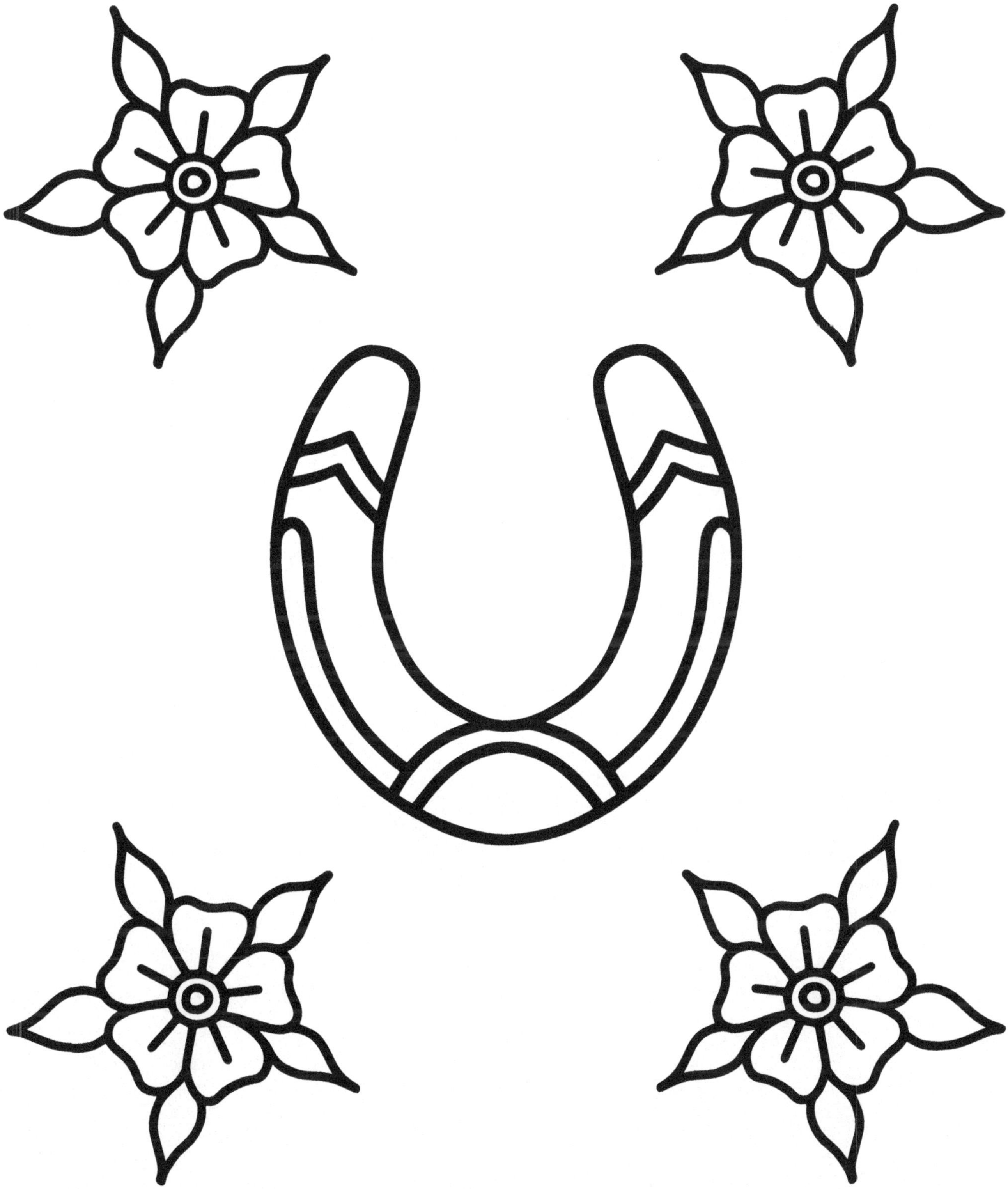

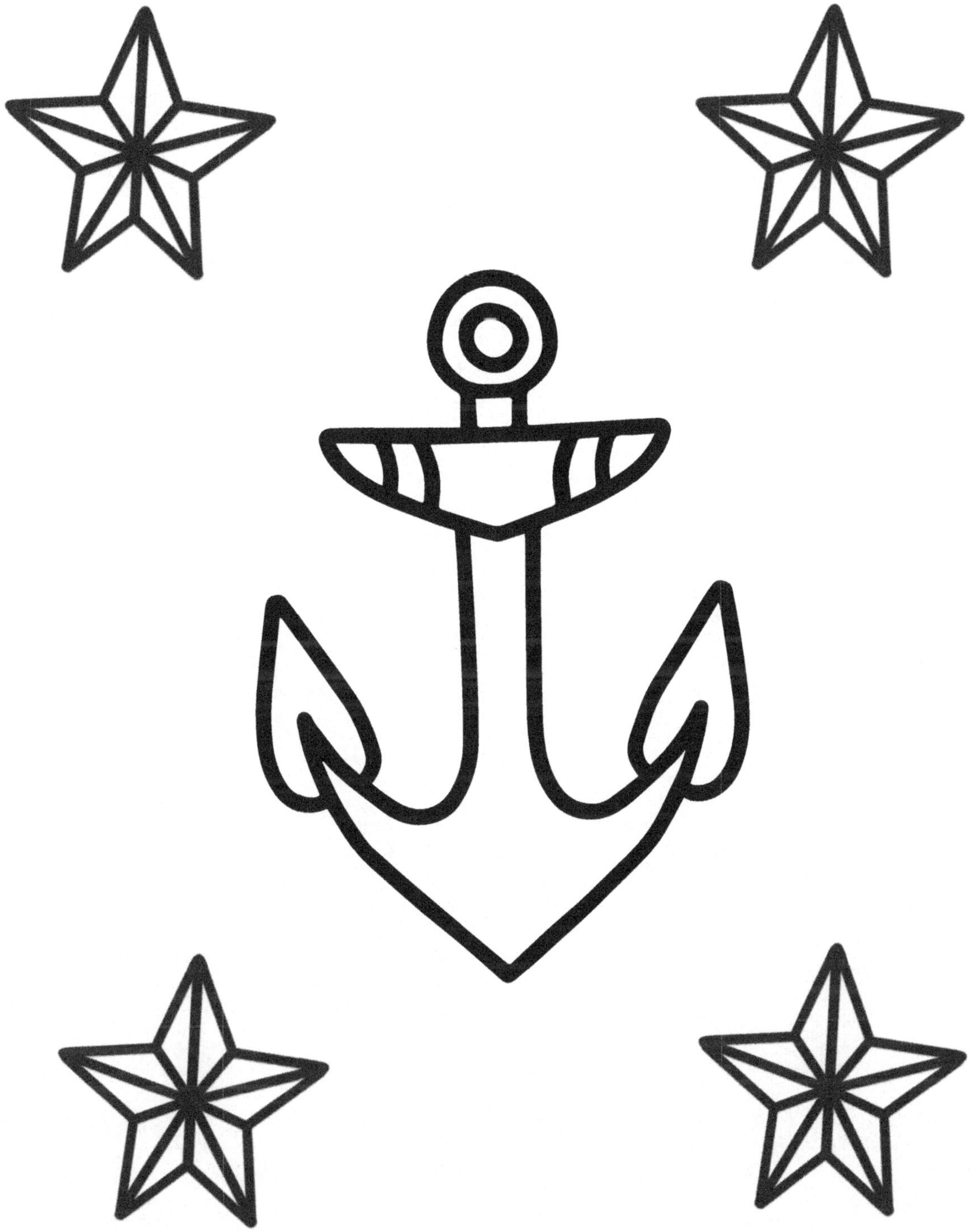

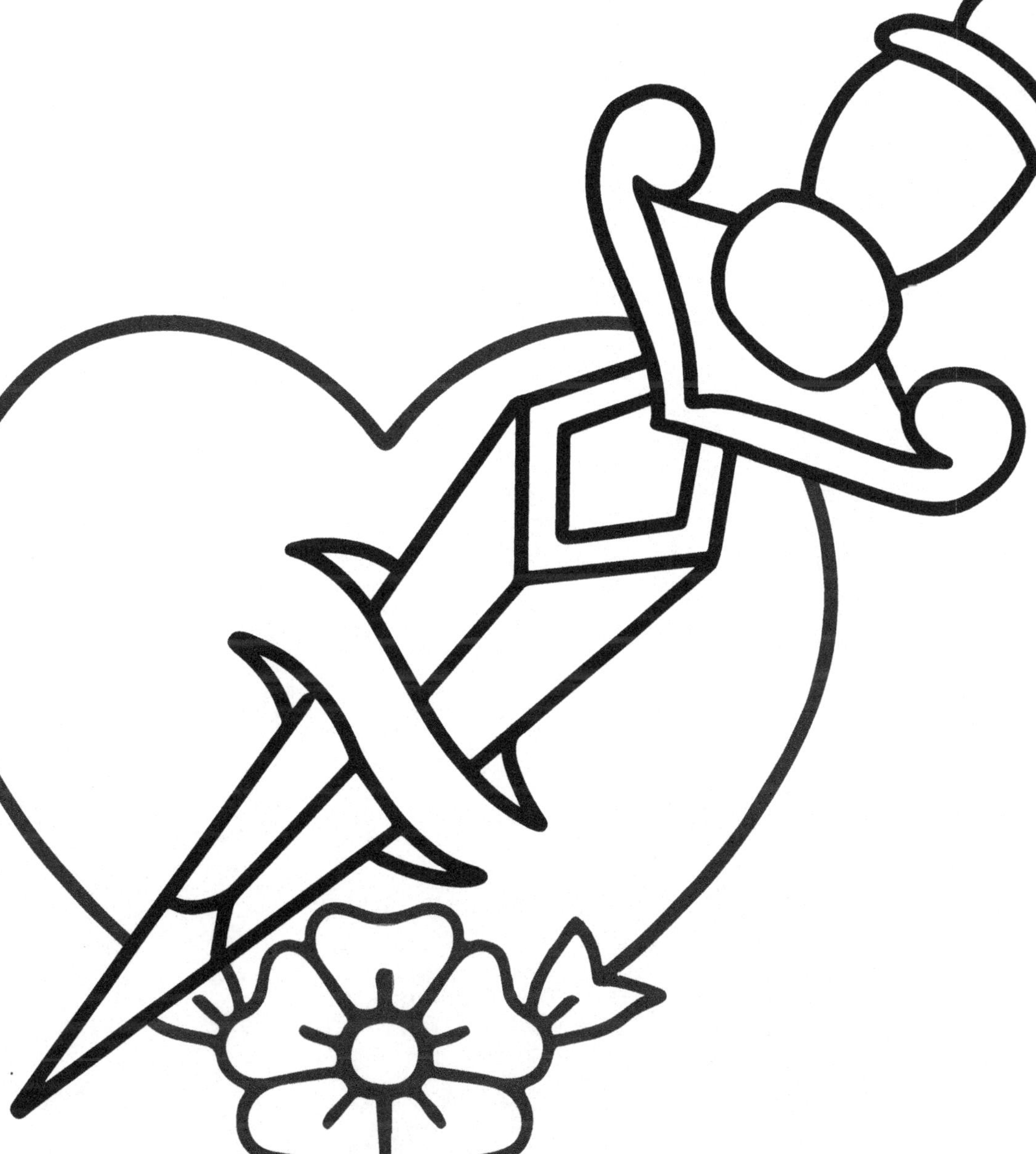

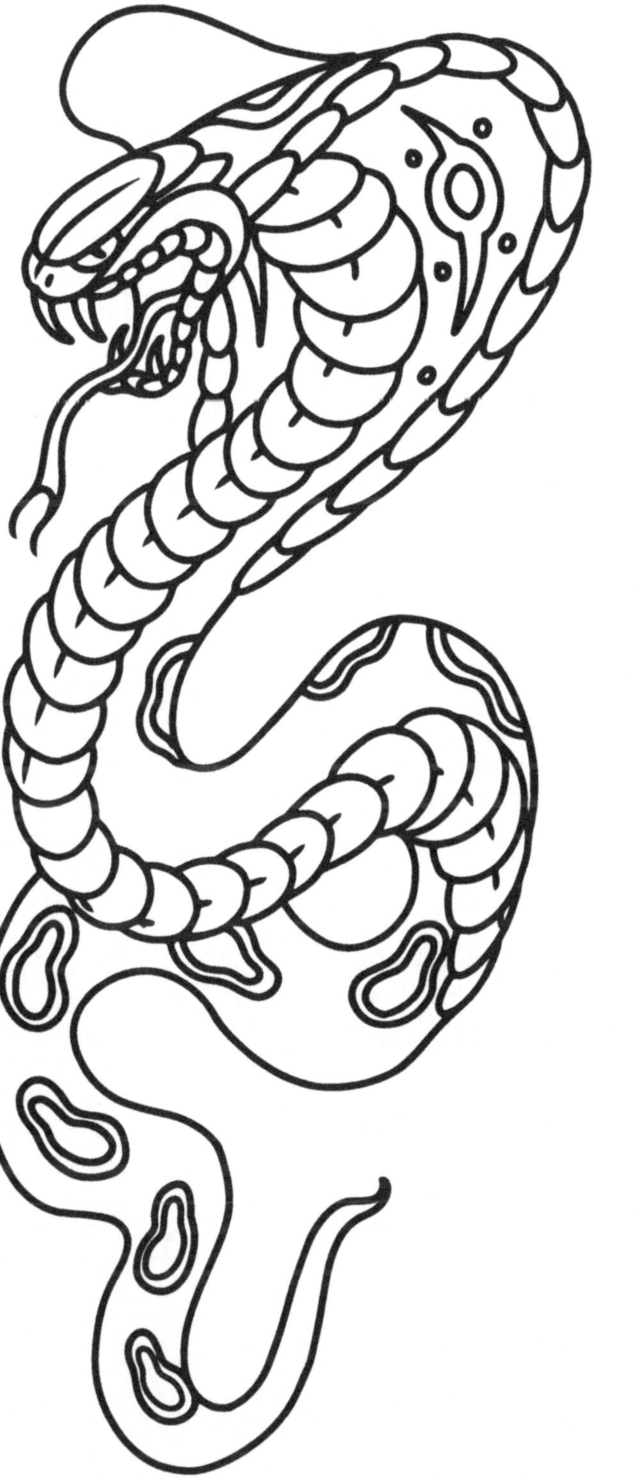

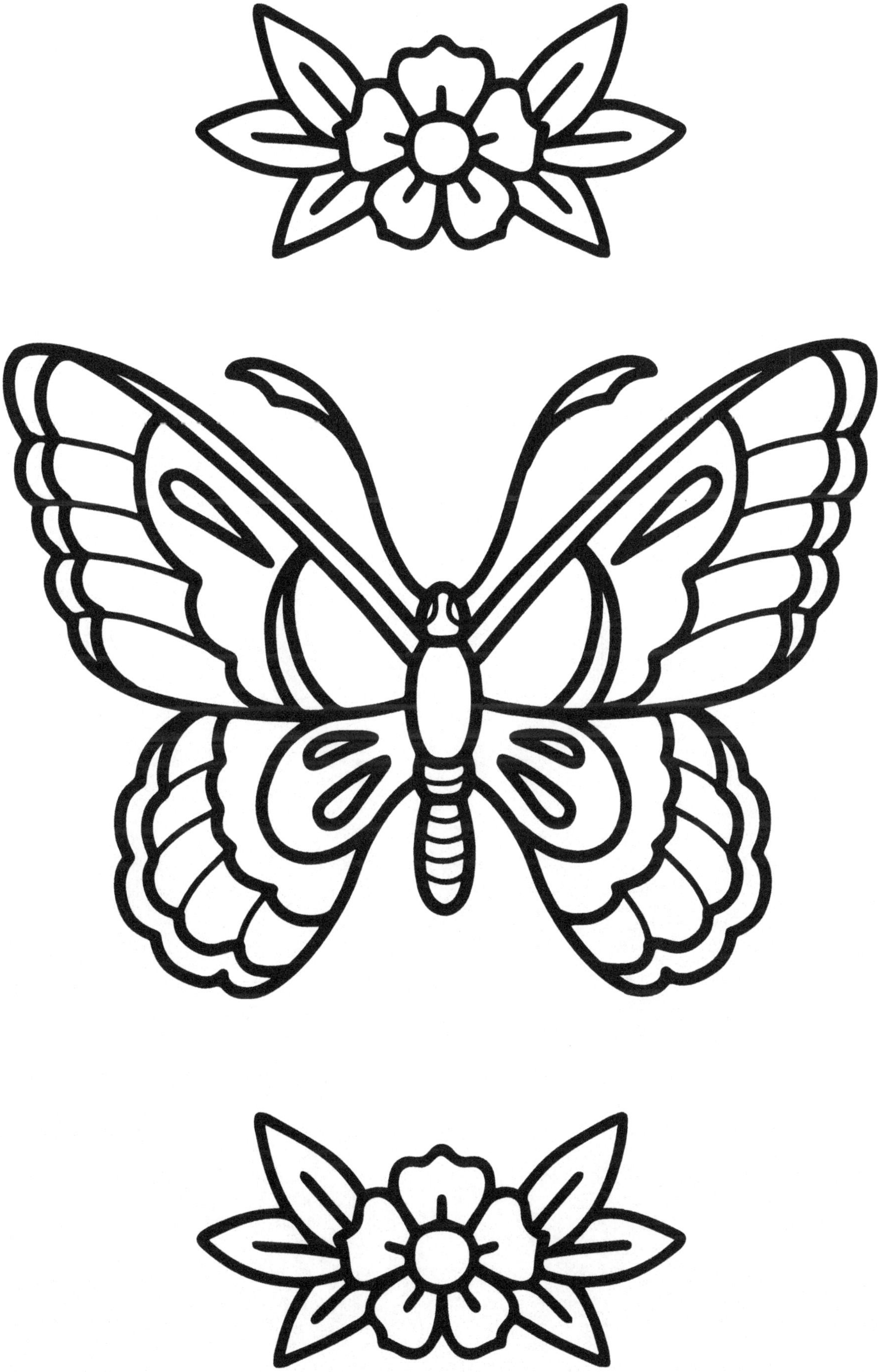